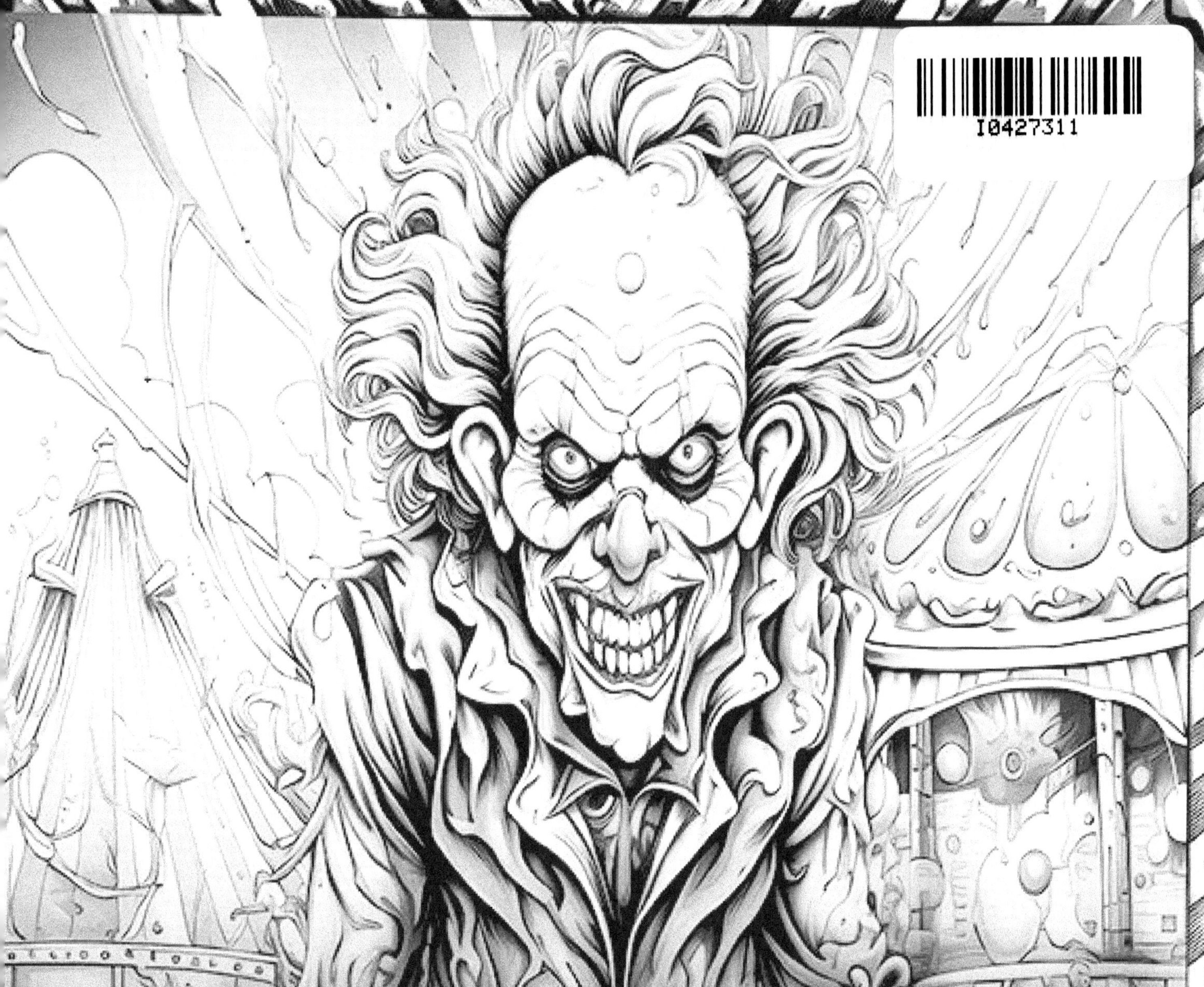

NIGHTMARE CIRCUS

A Terrifying Clown Coloring Experience

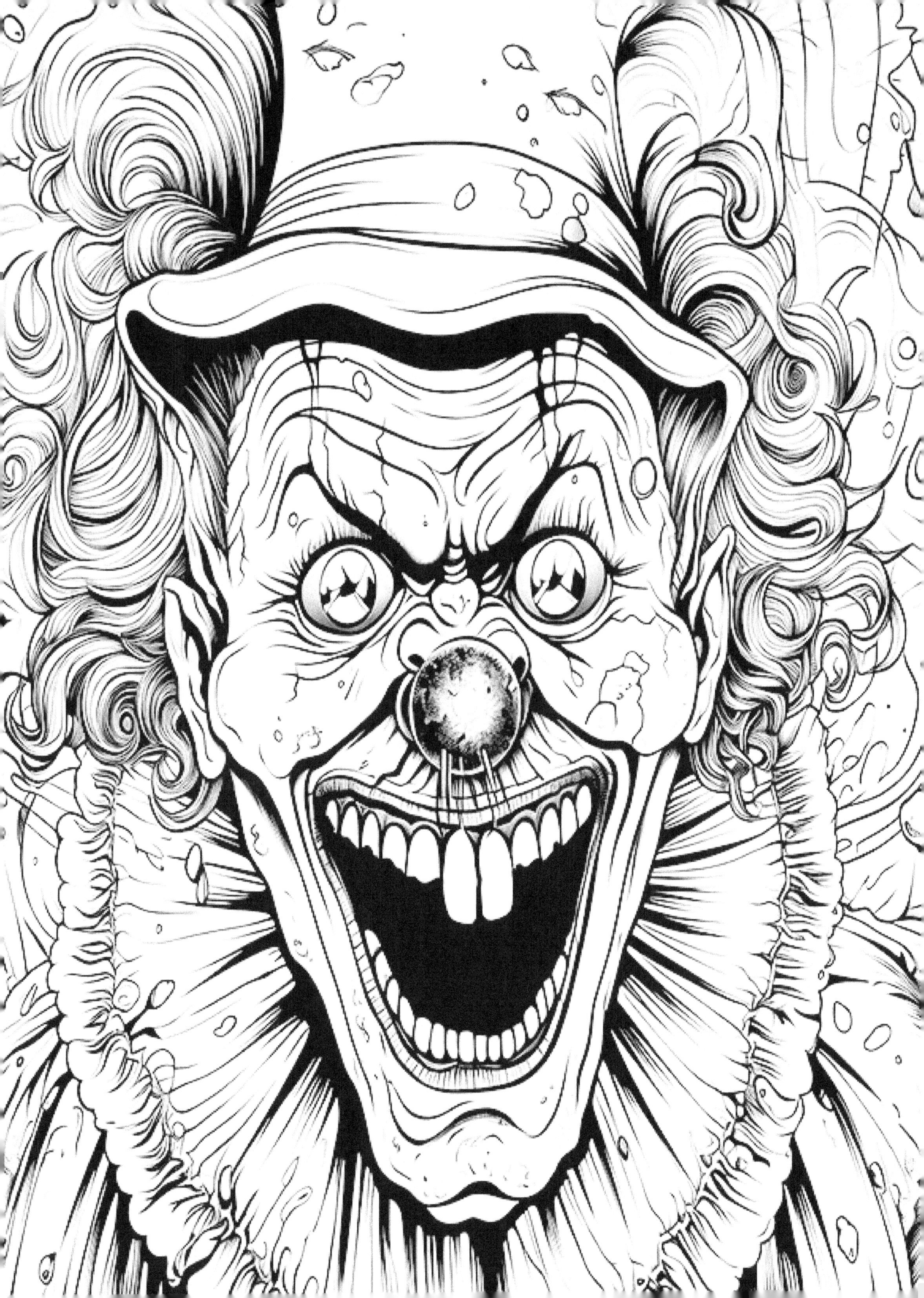

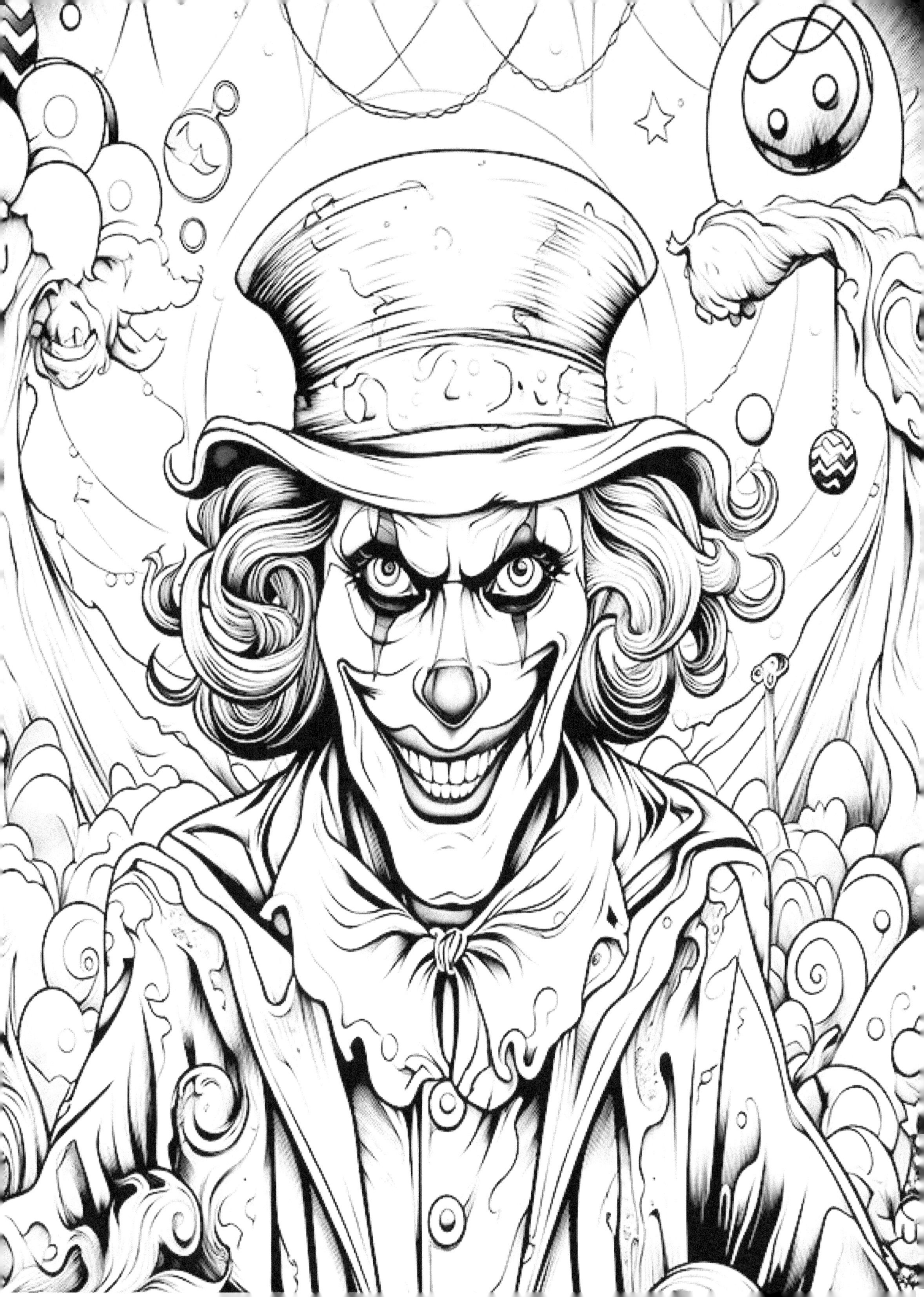

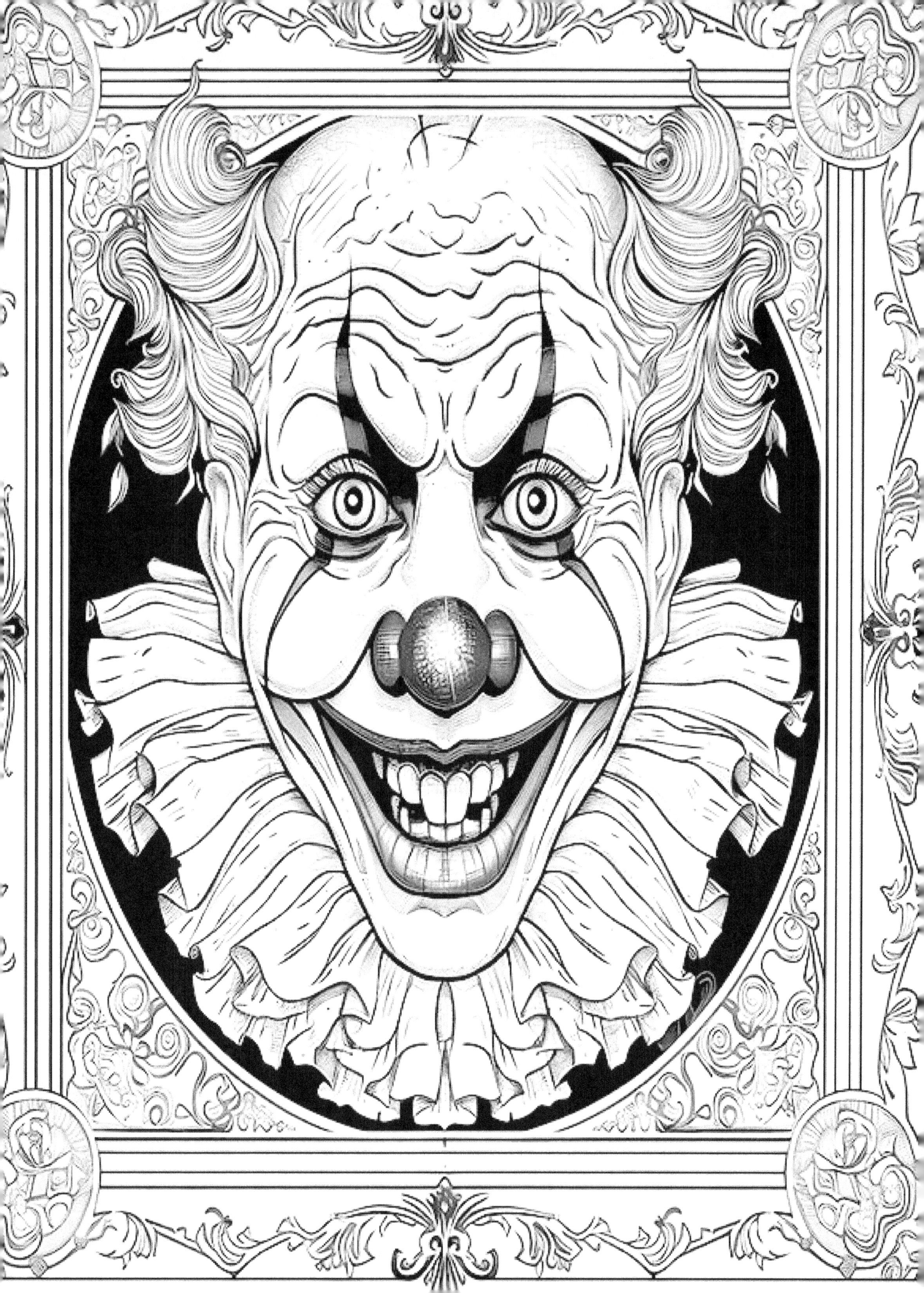

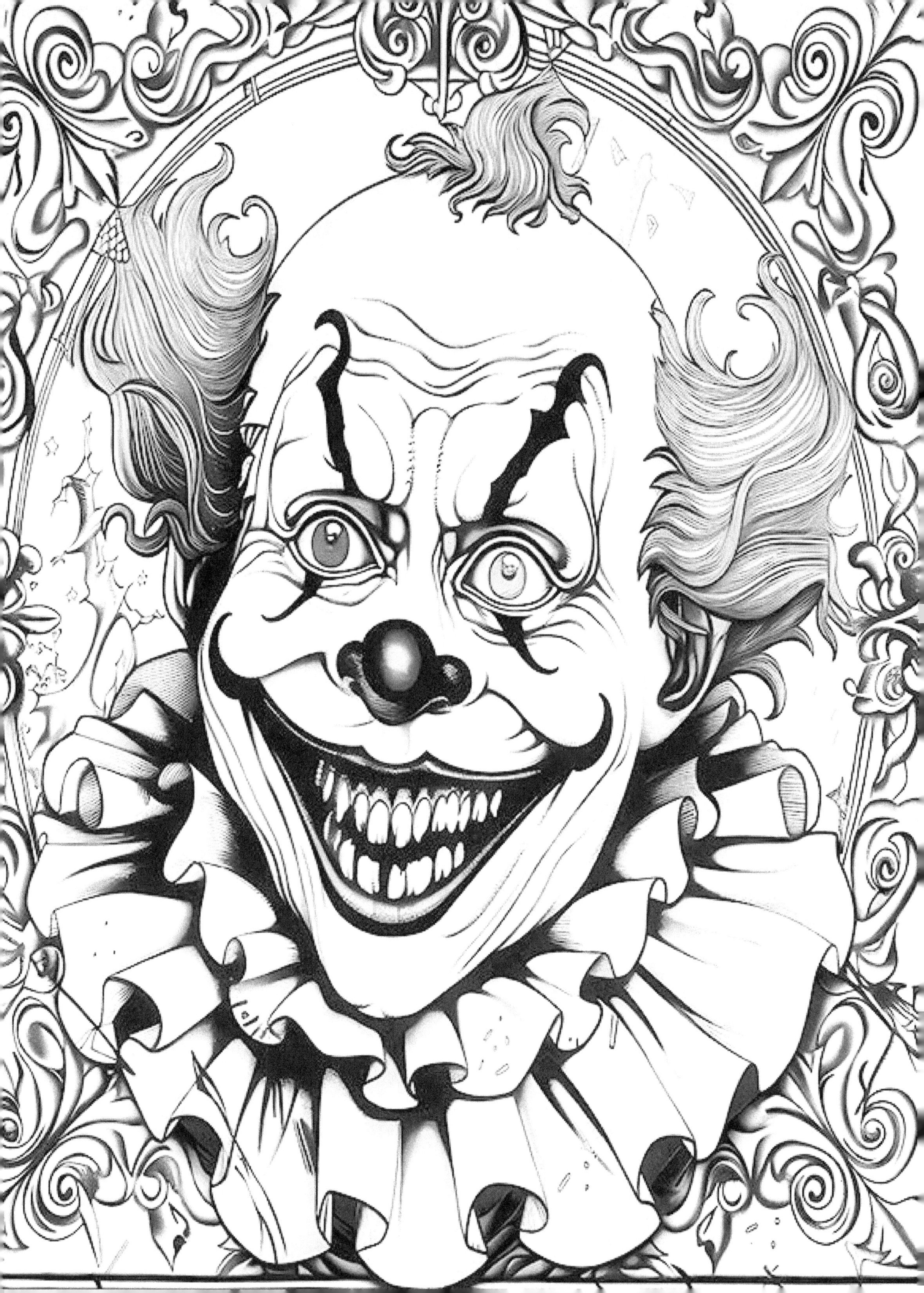

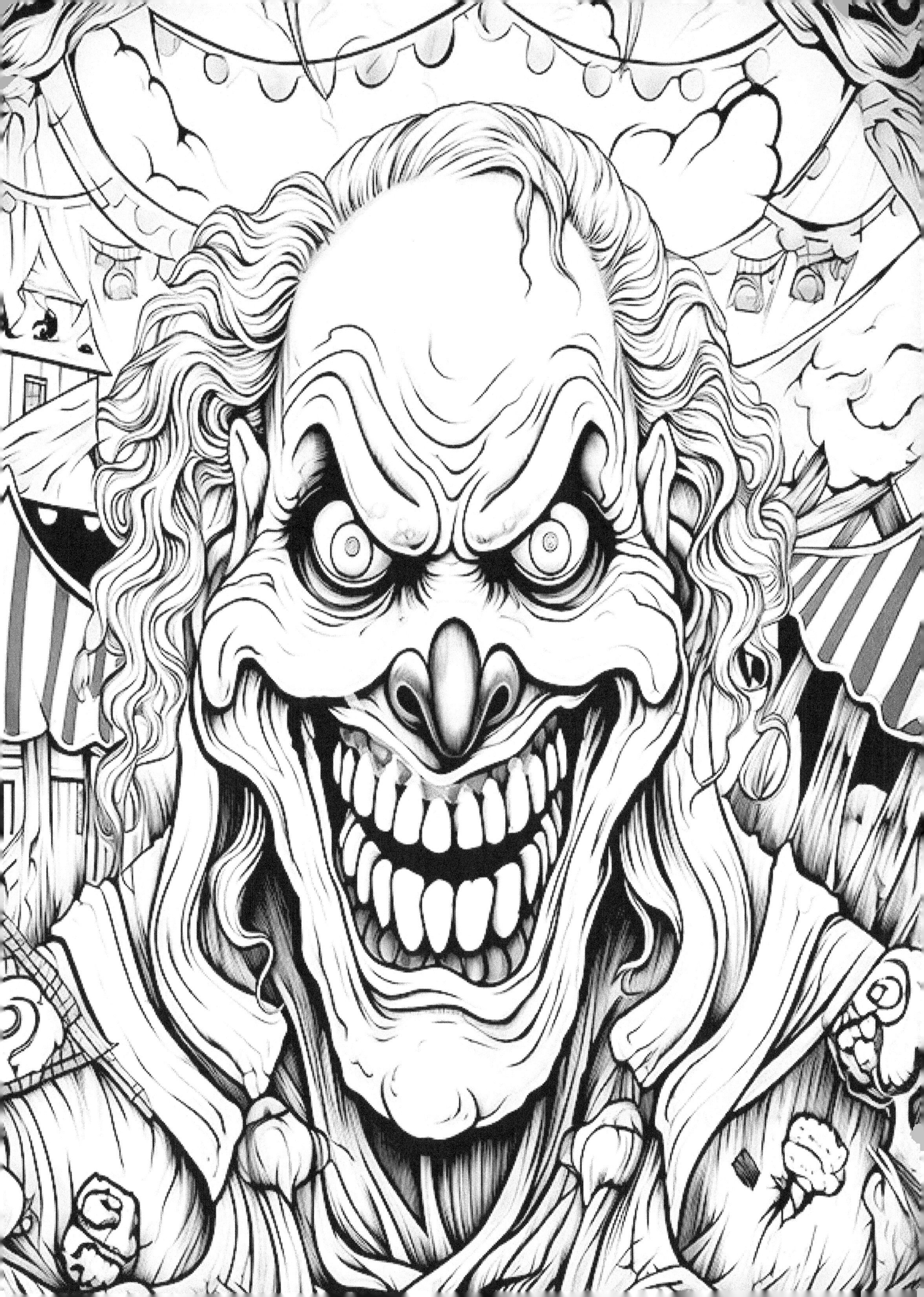

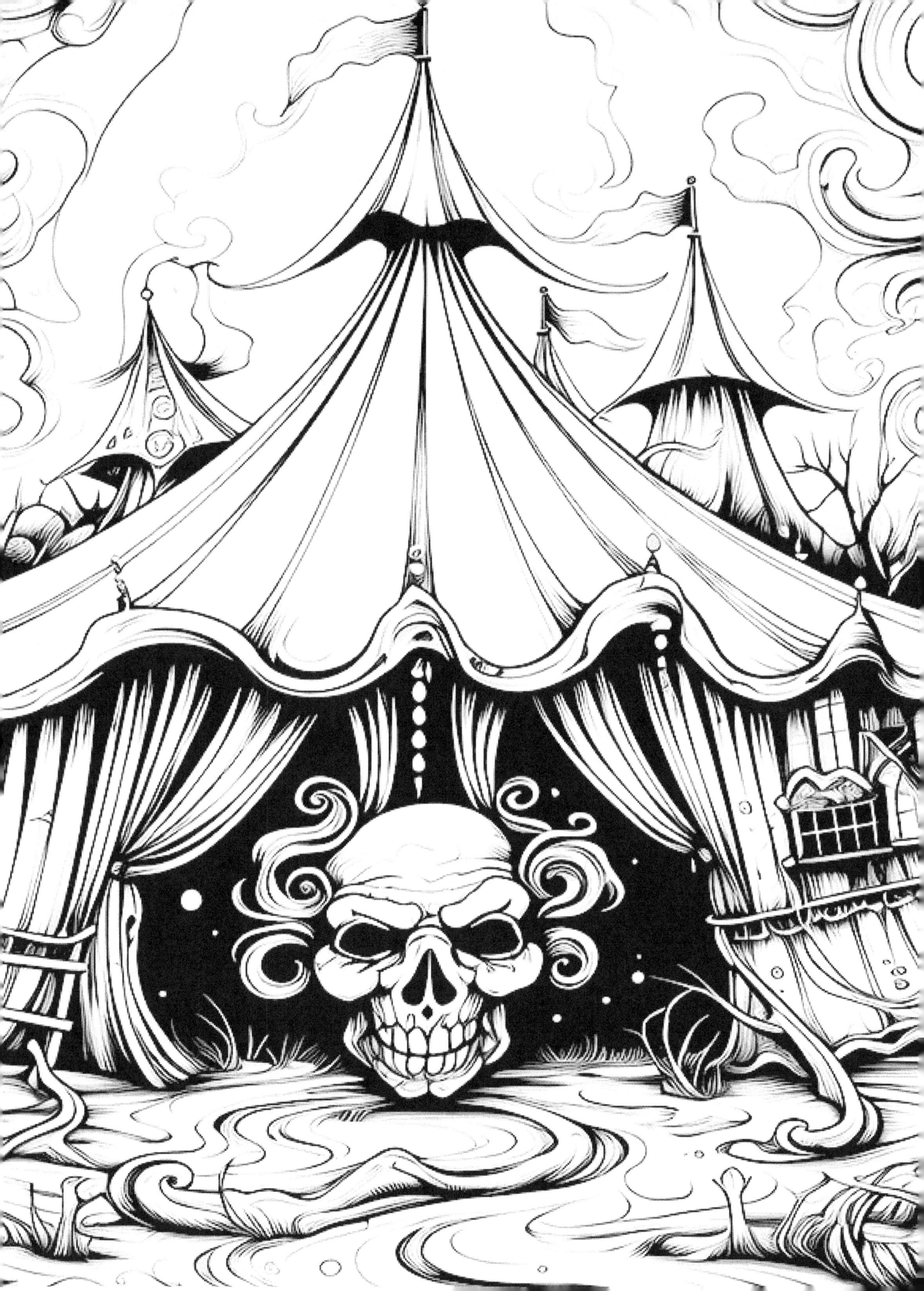

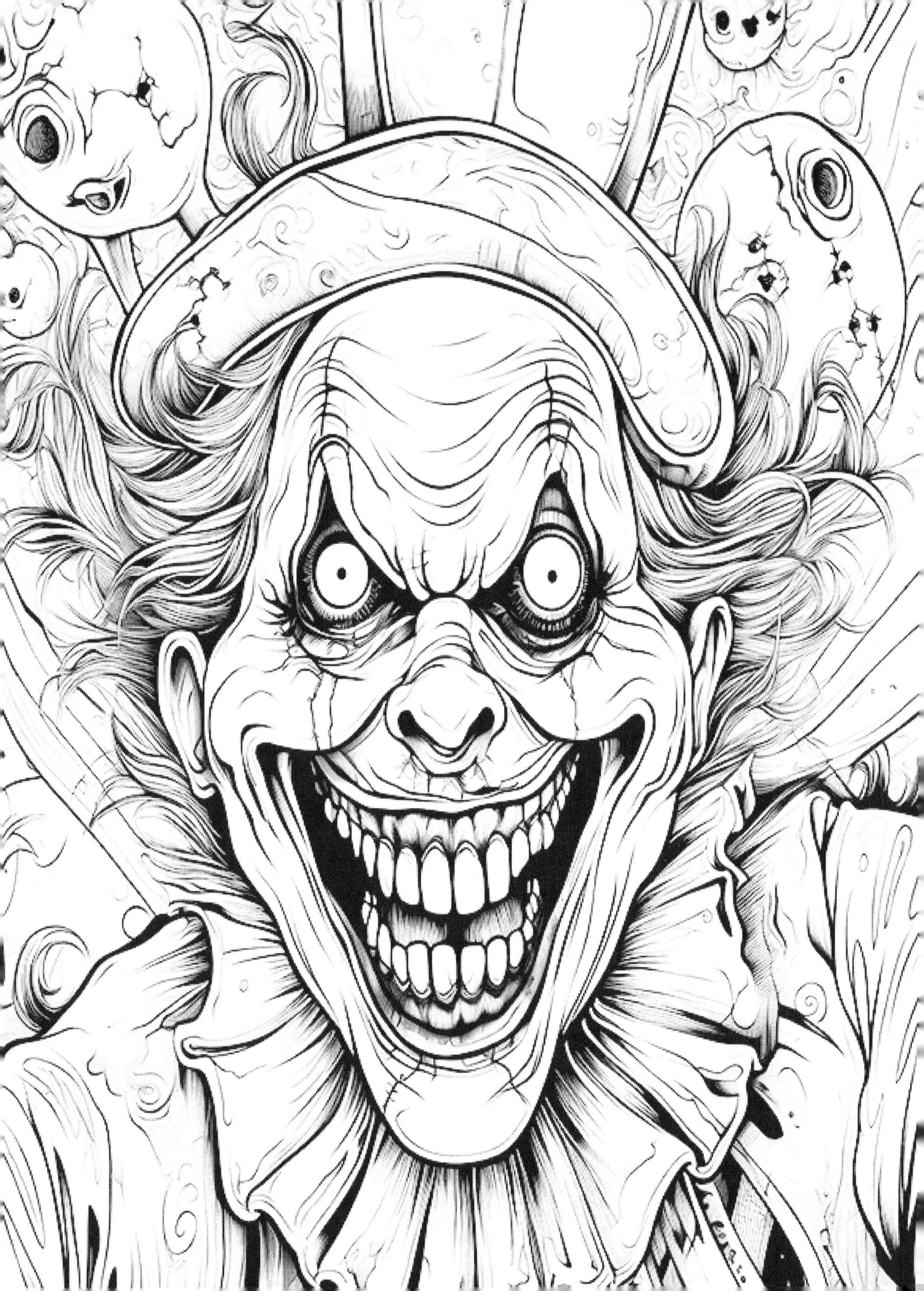

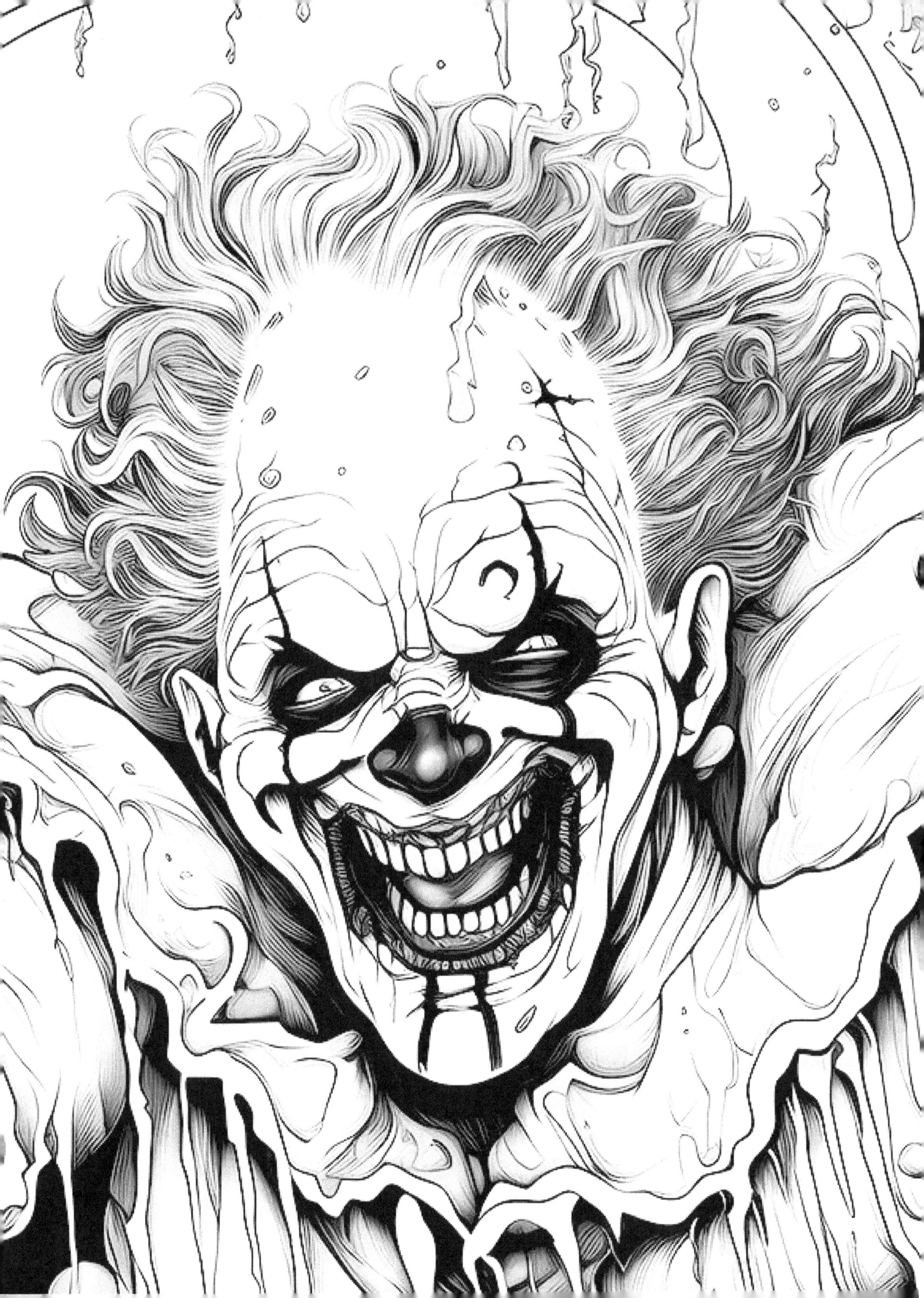

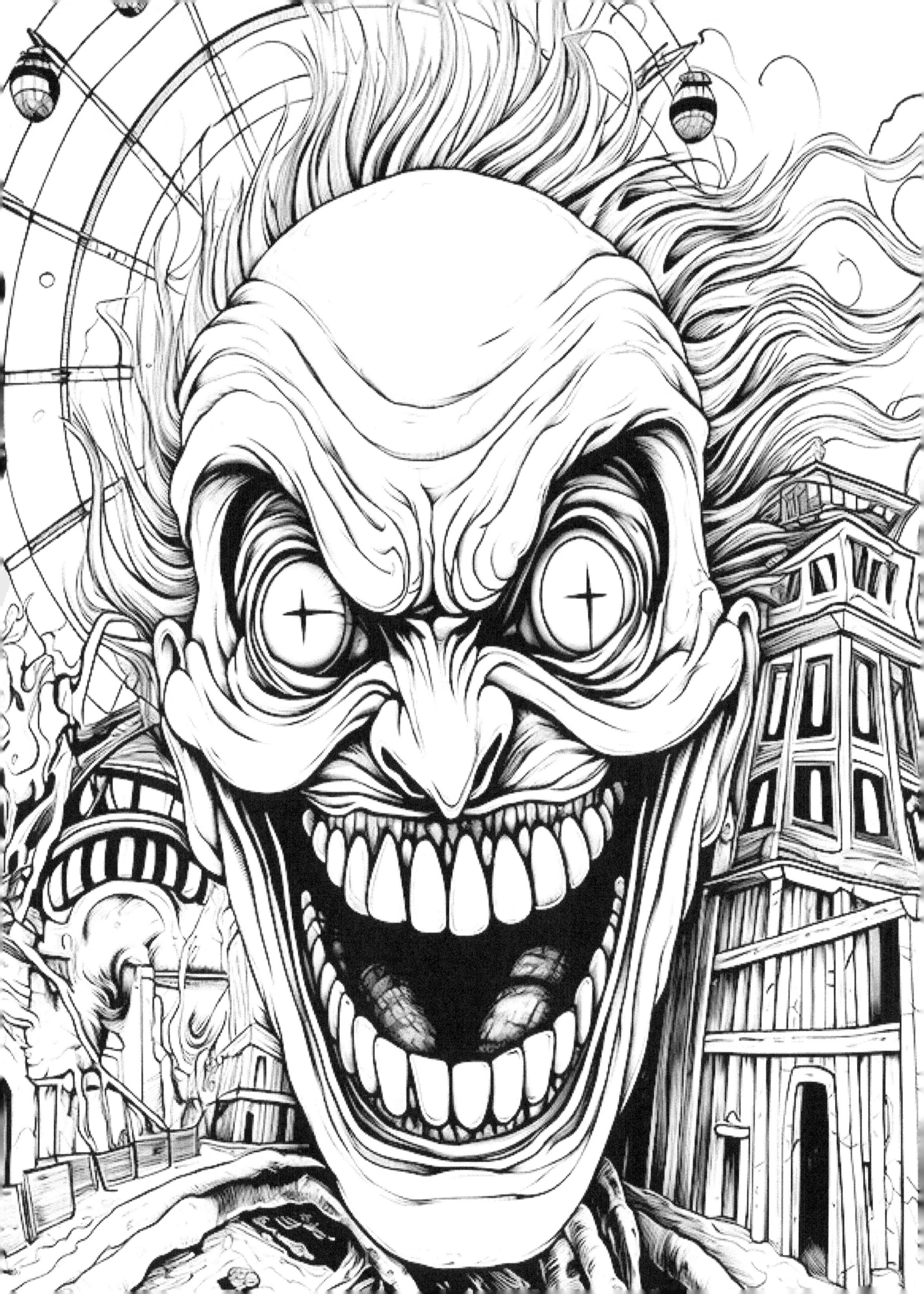

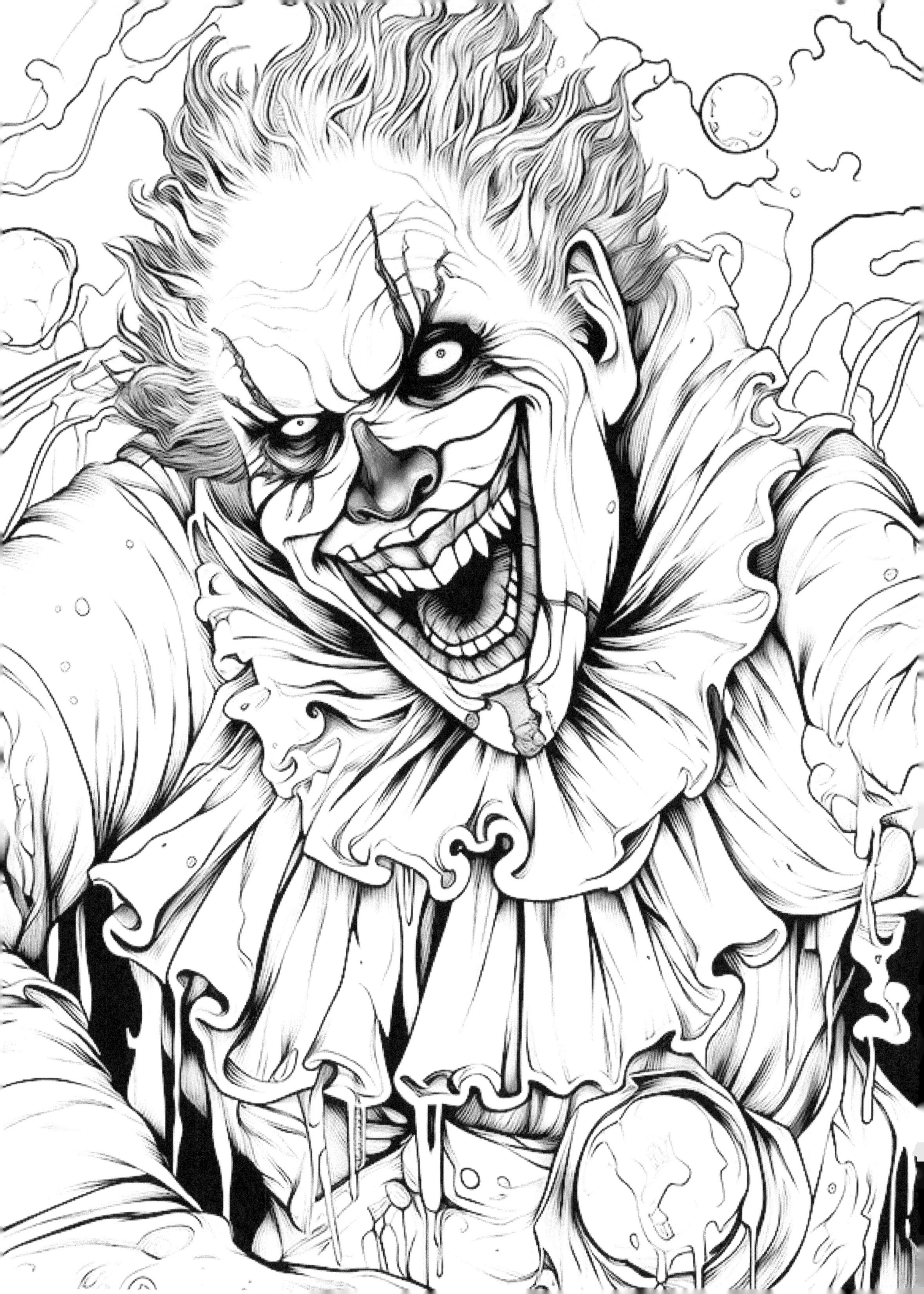

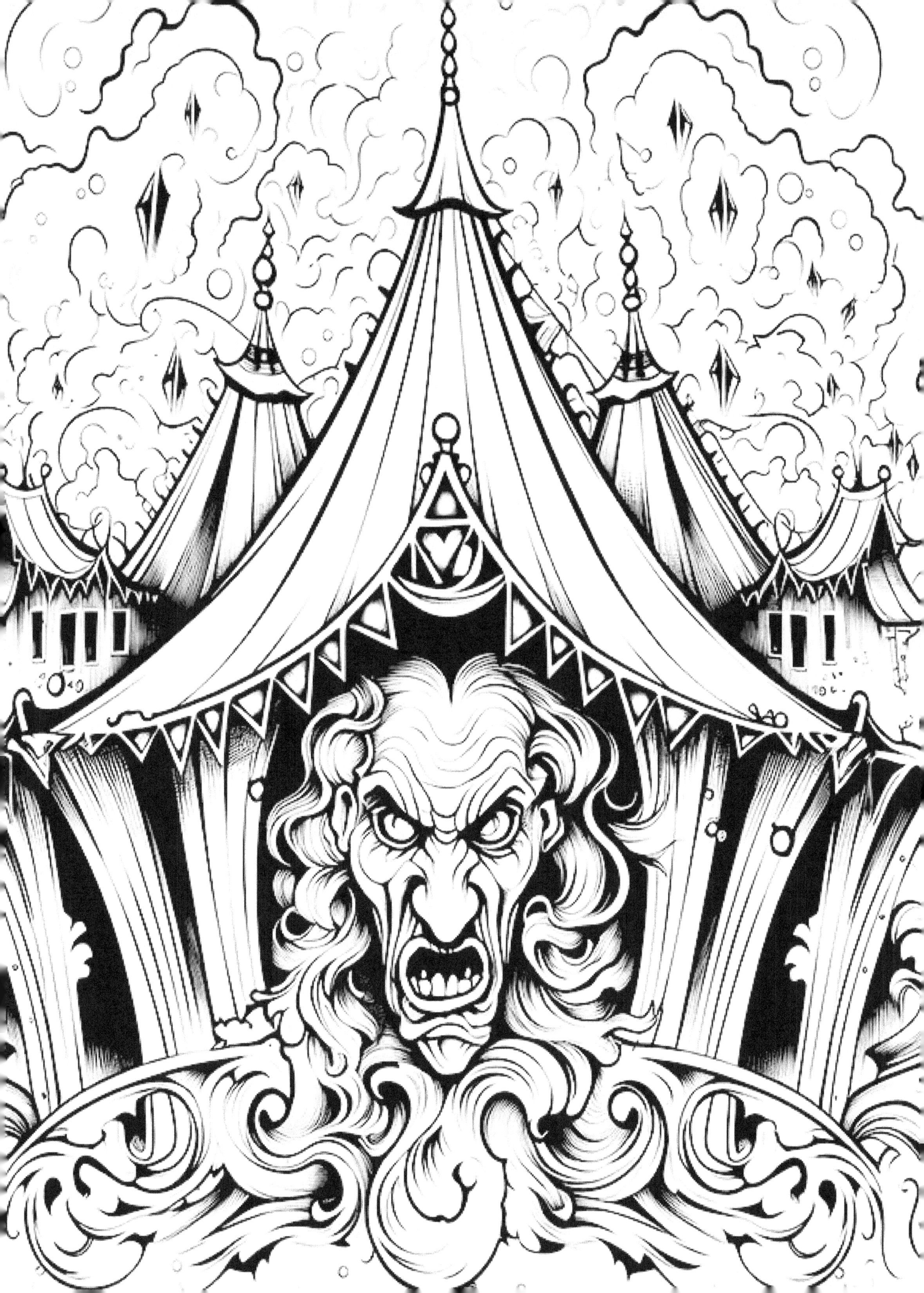

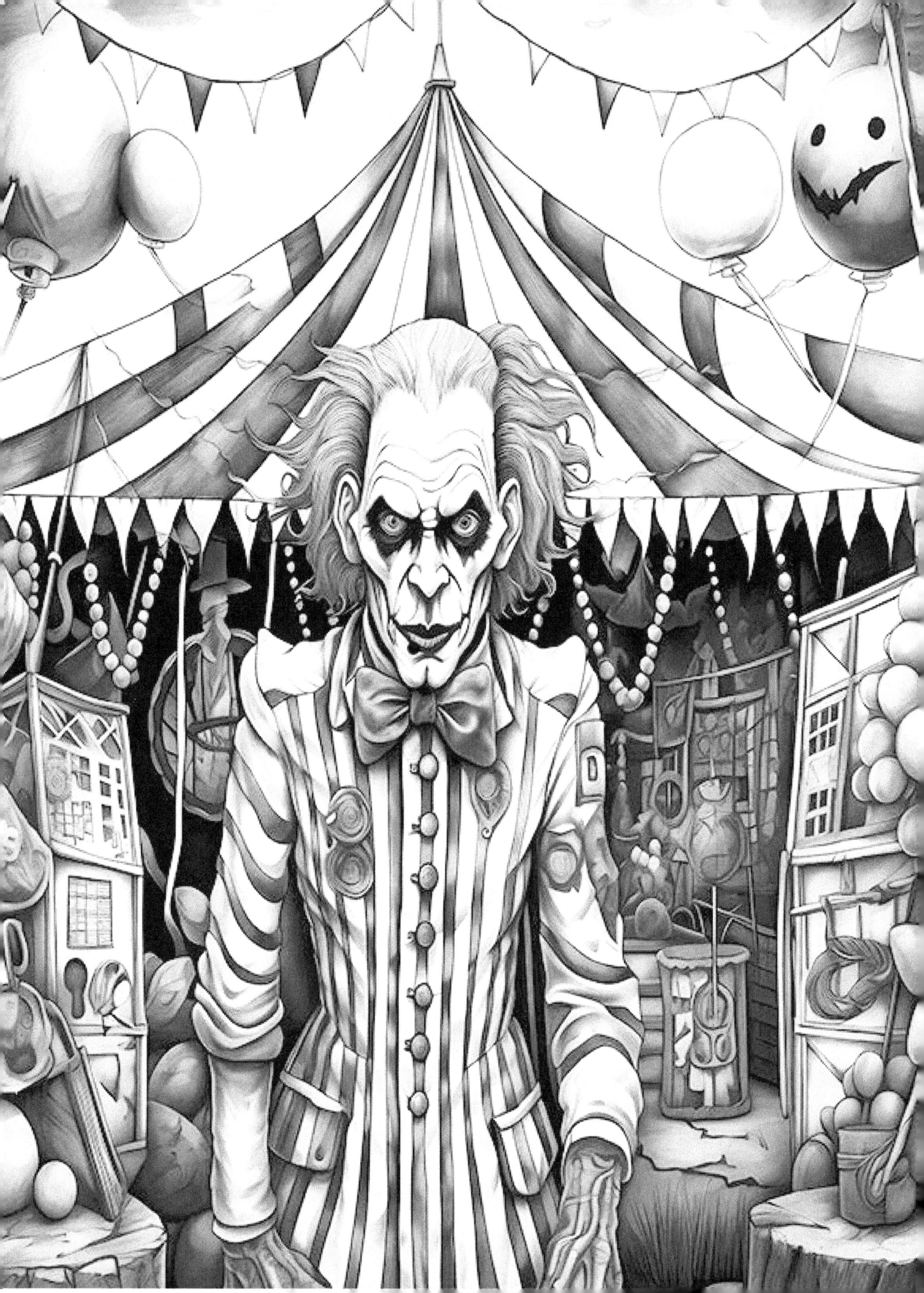

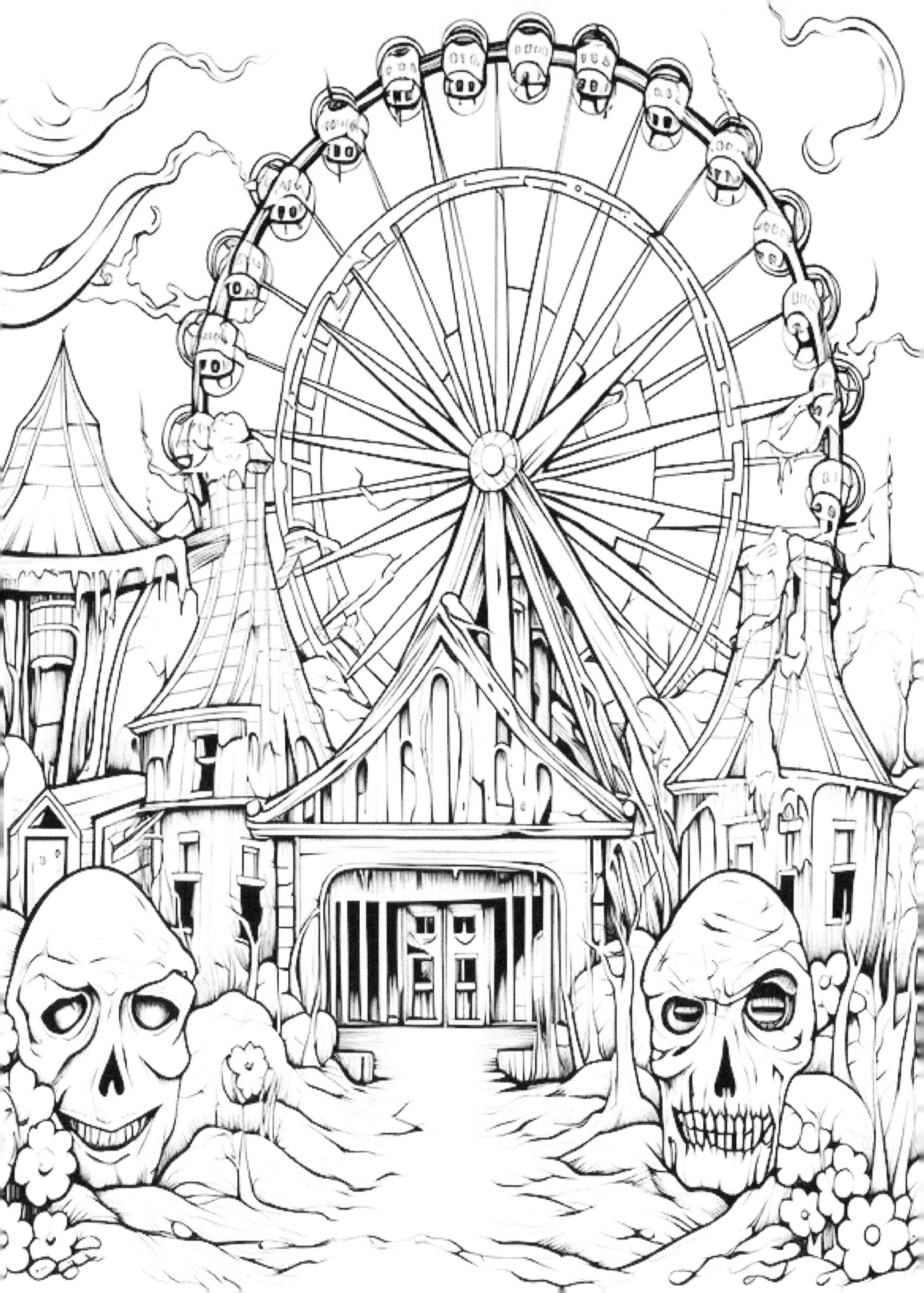

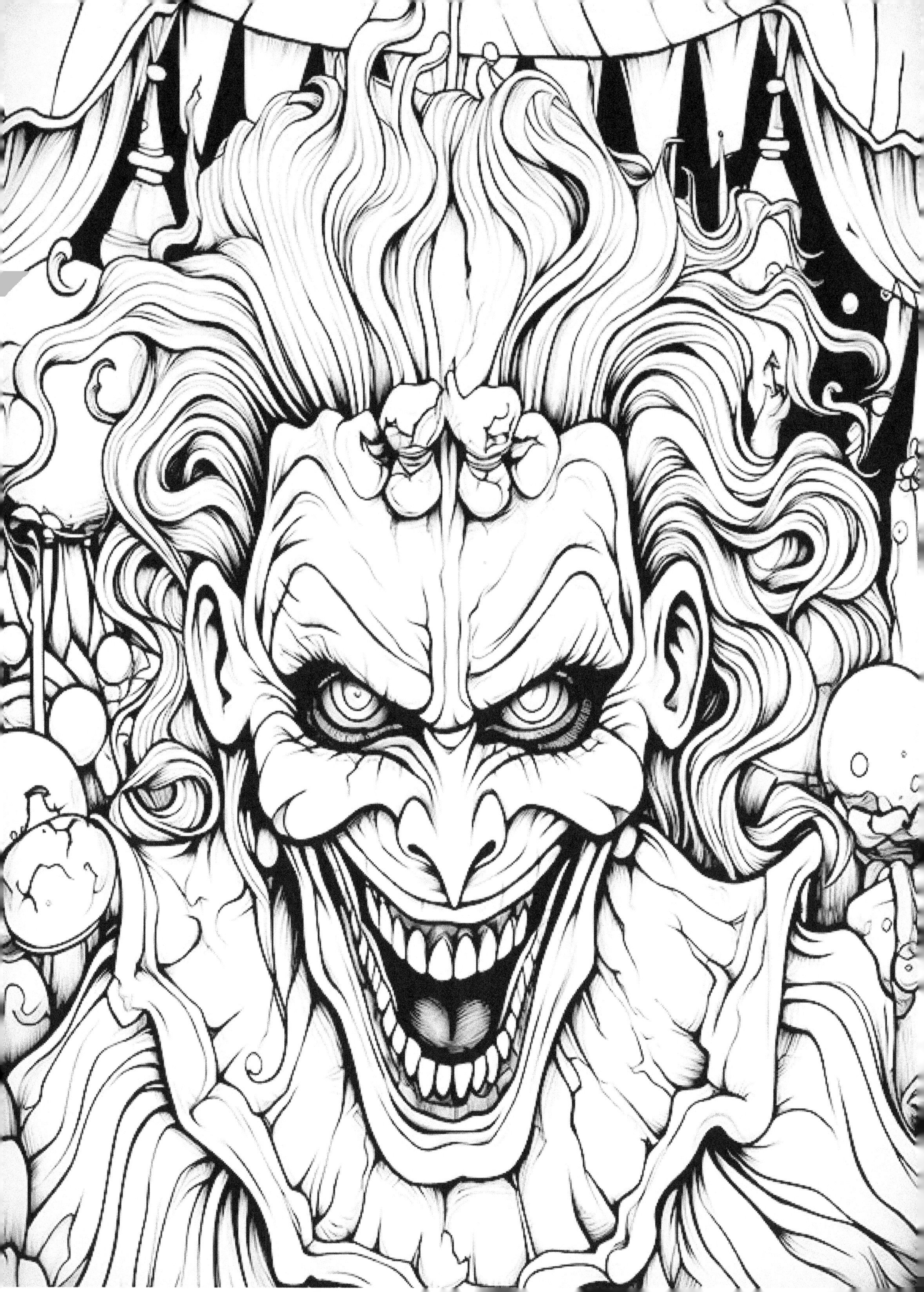

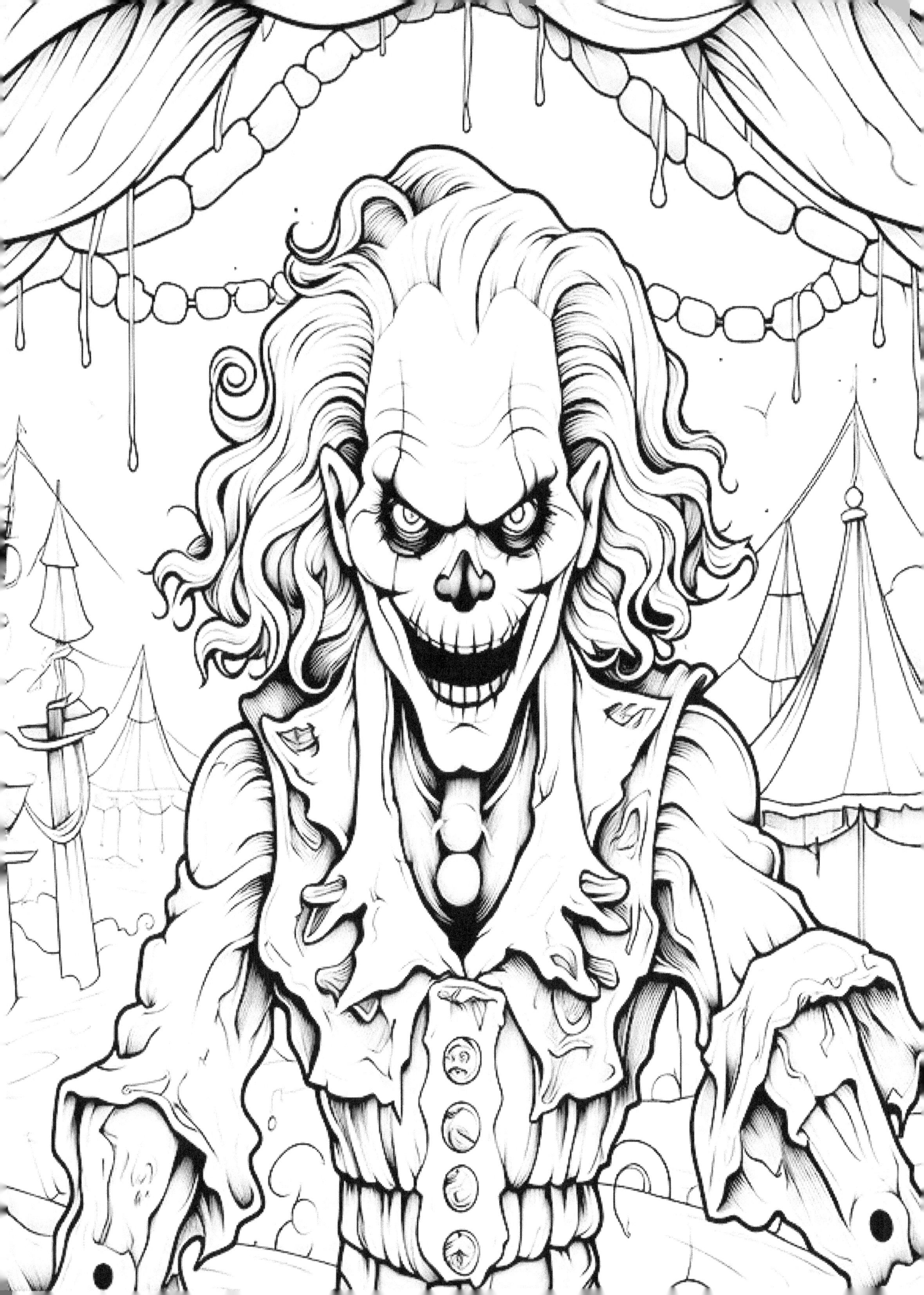

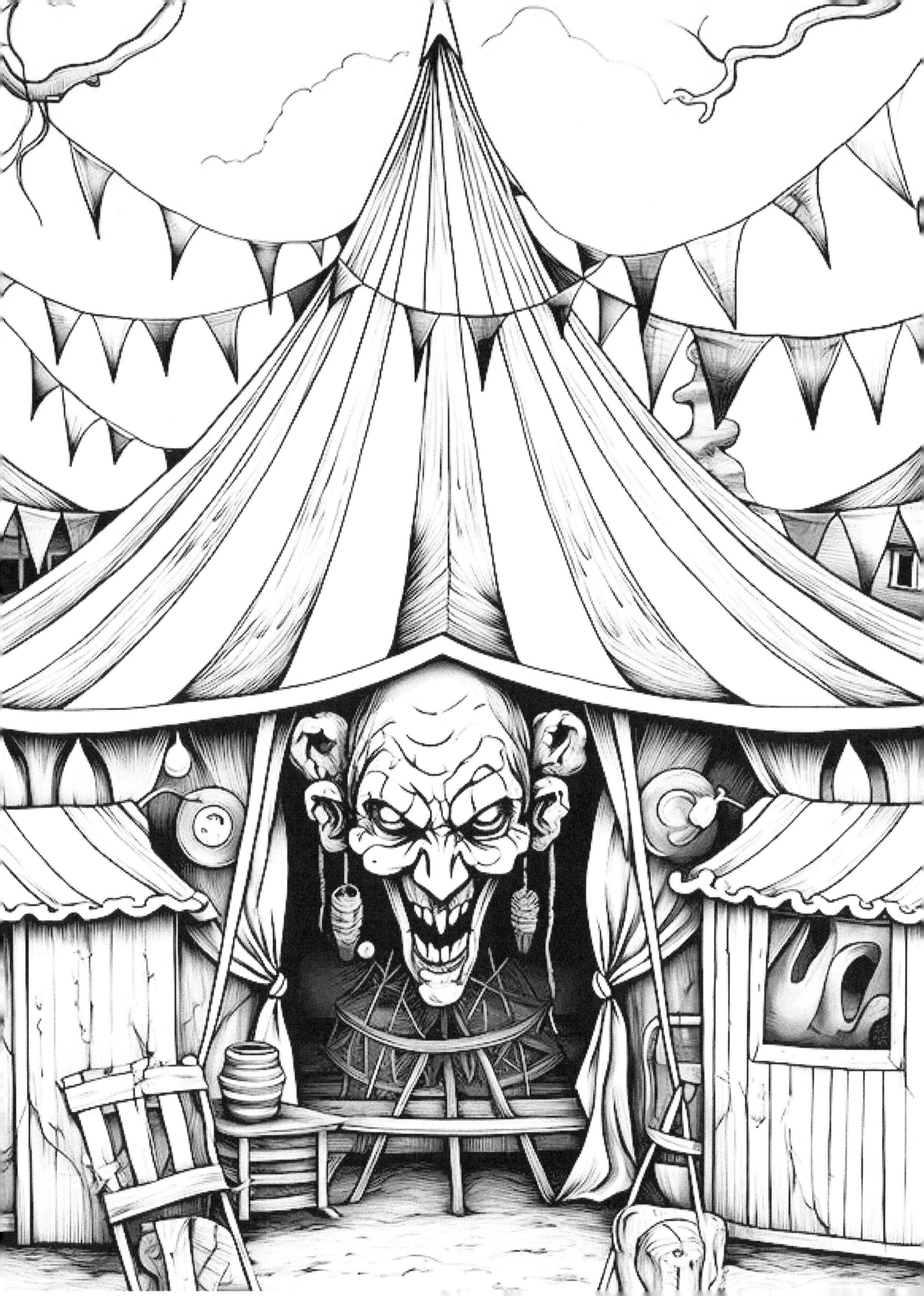

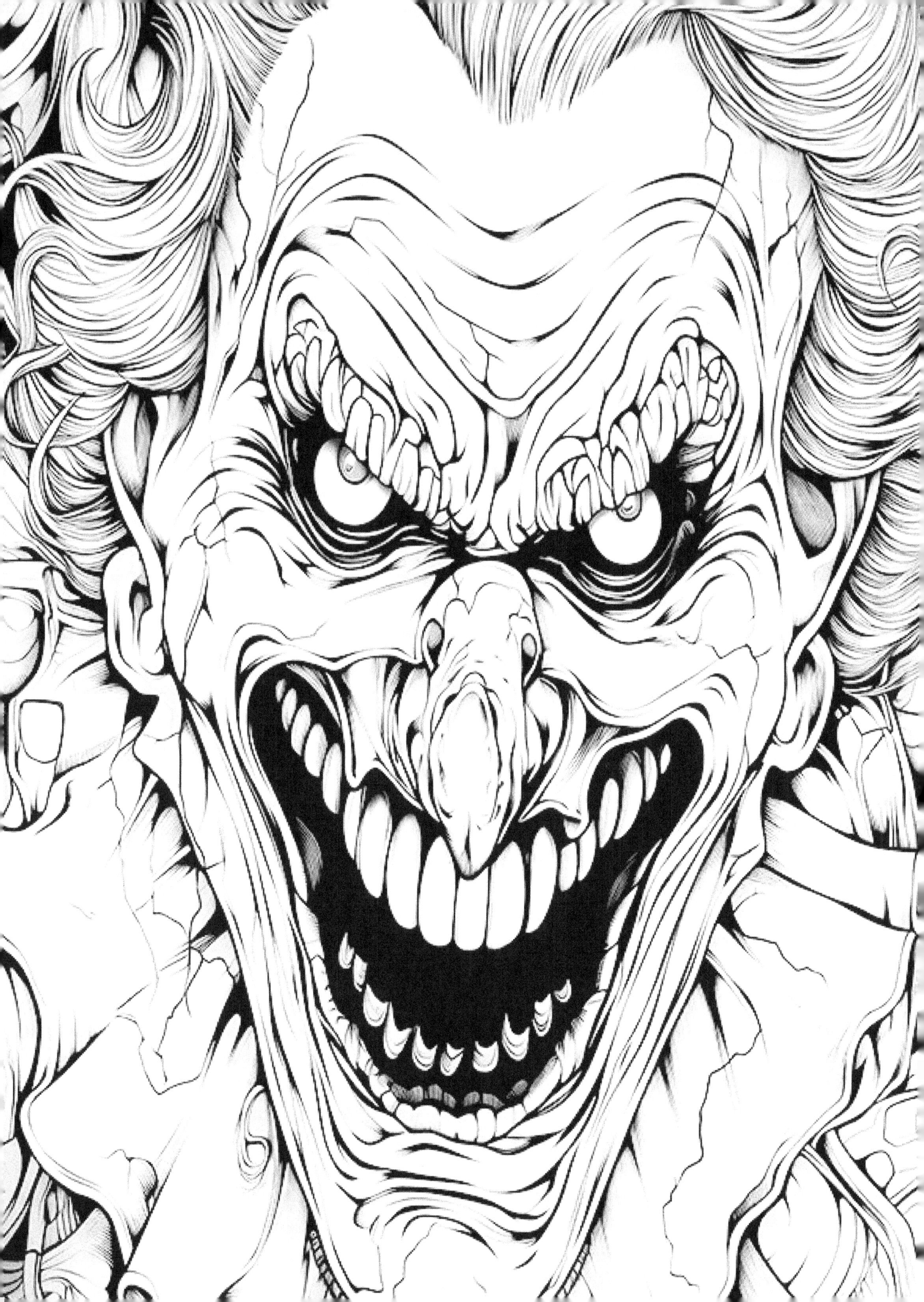

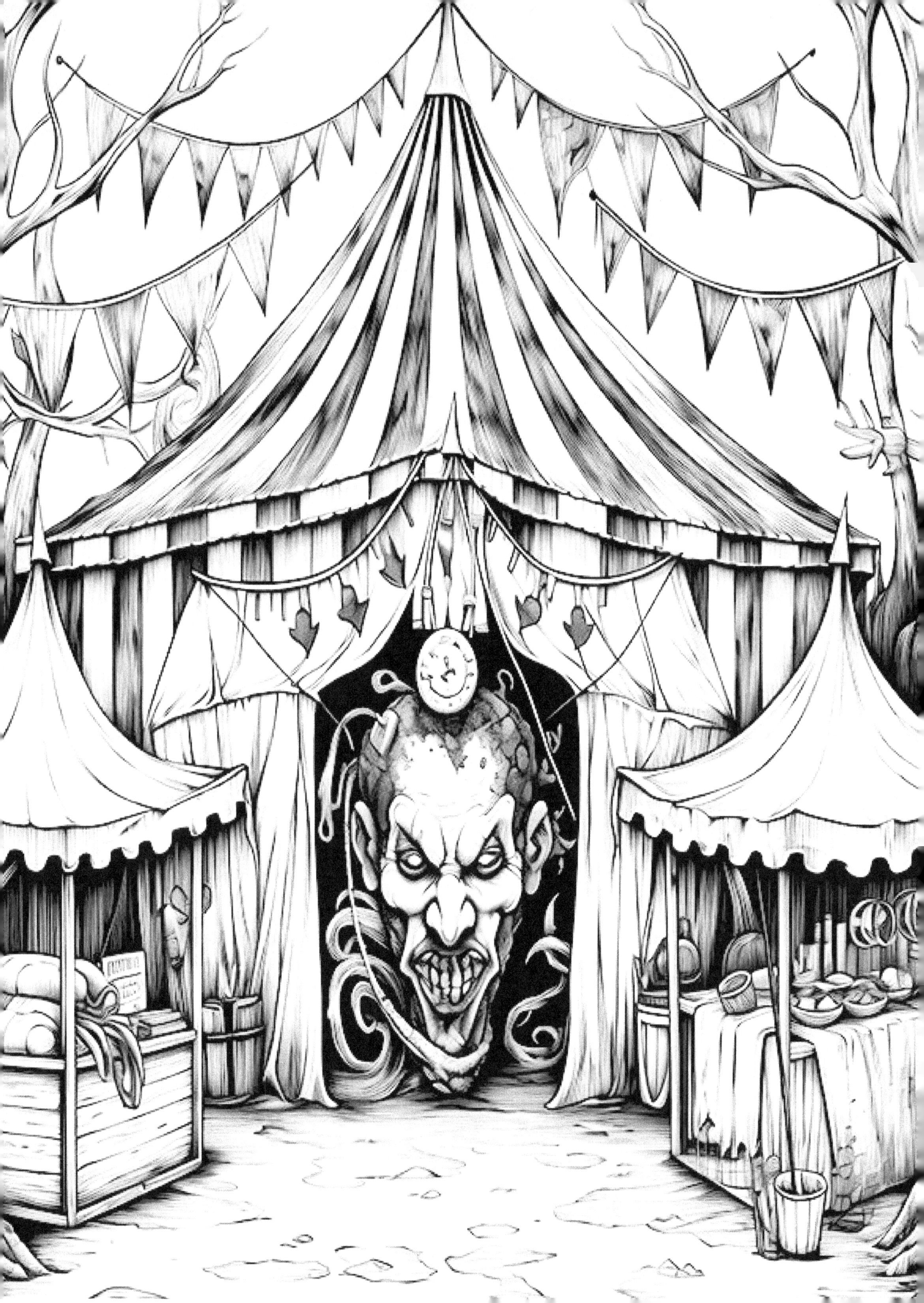

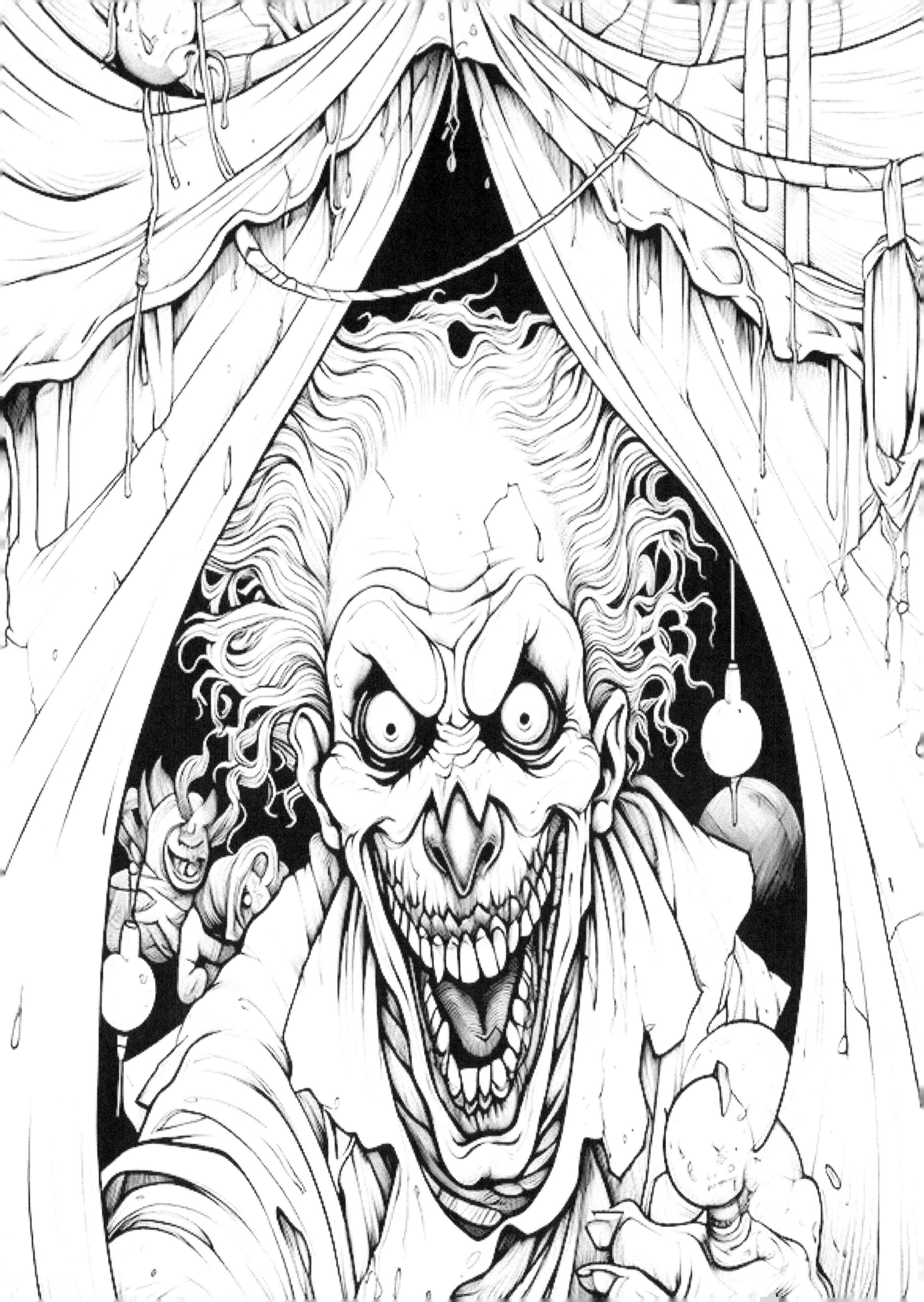

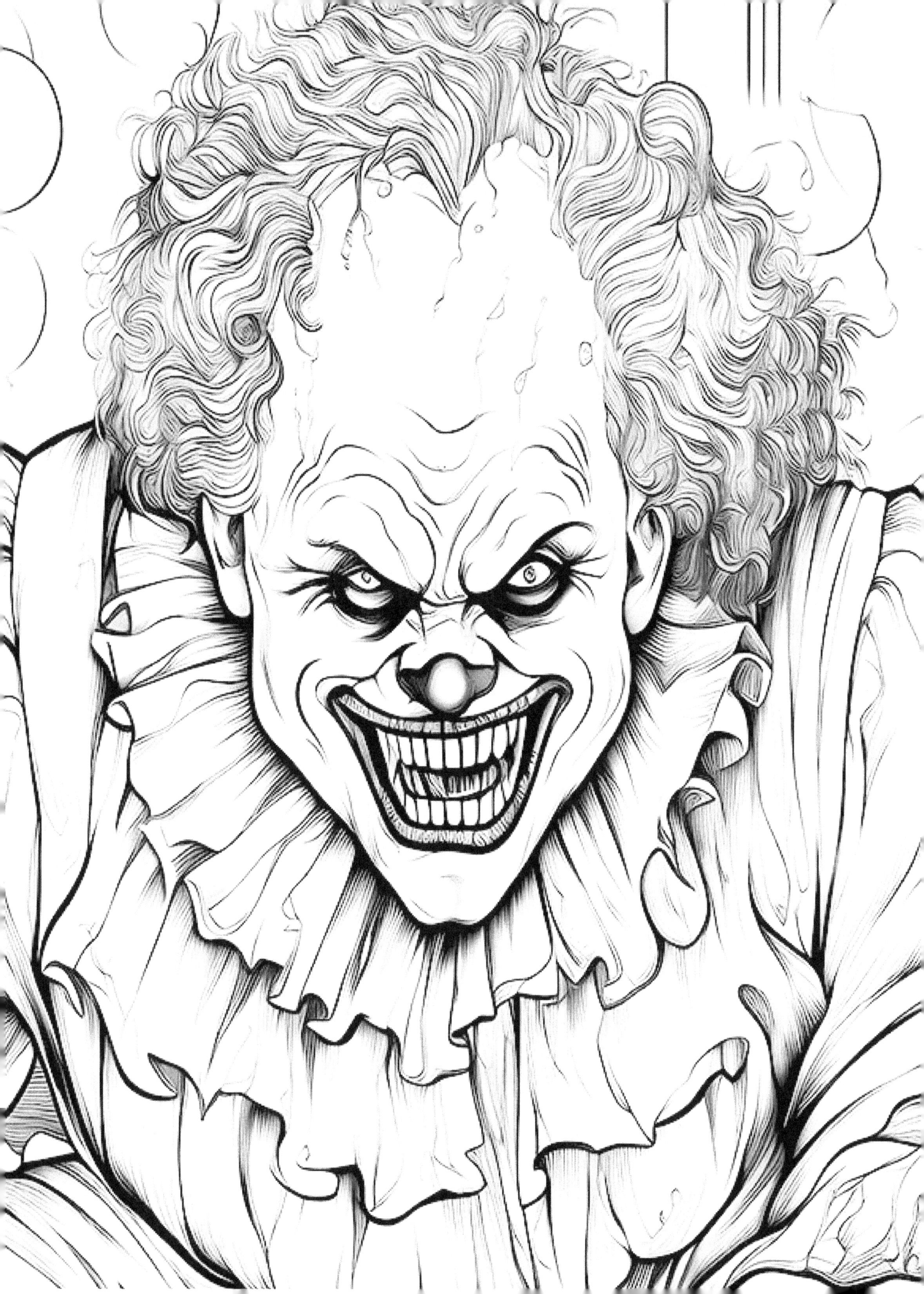

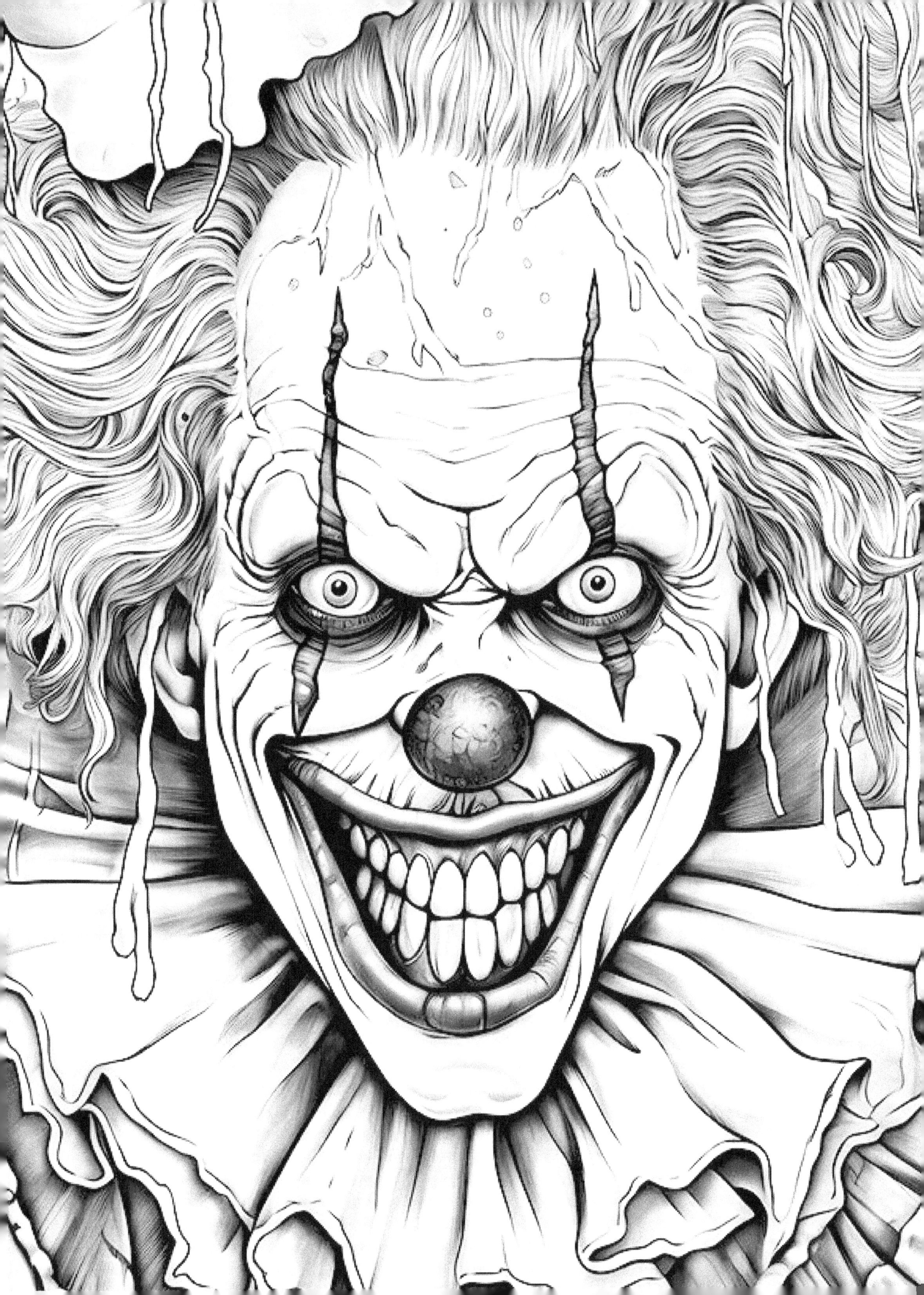

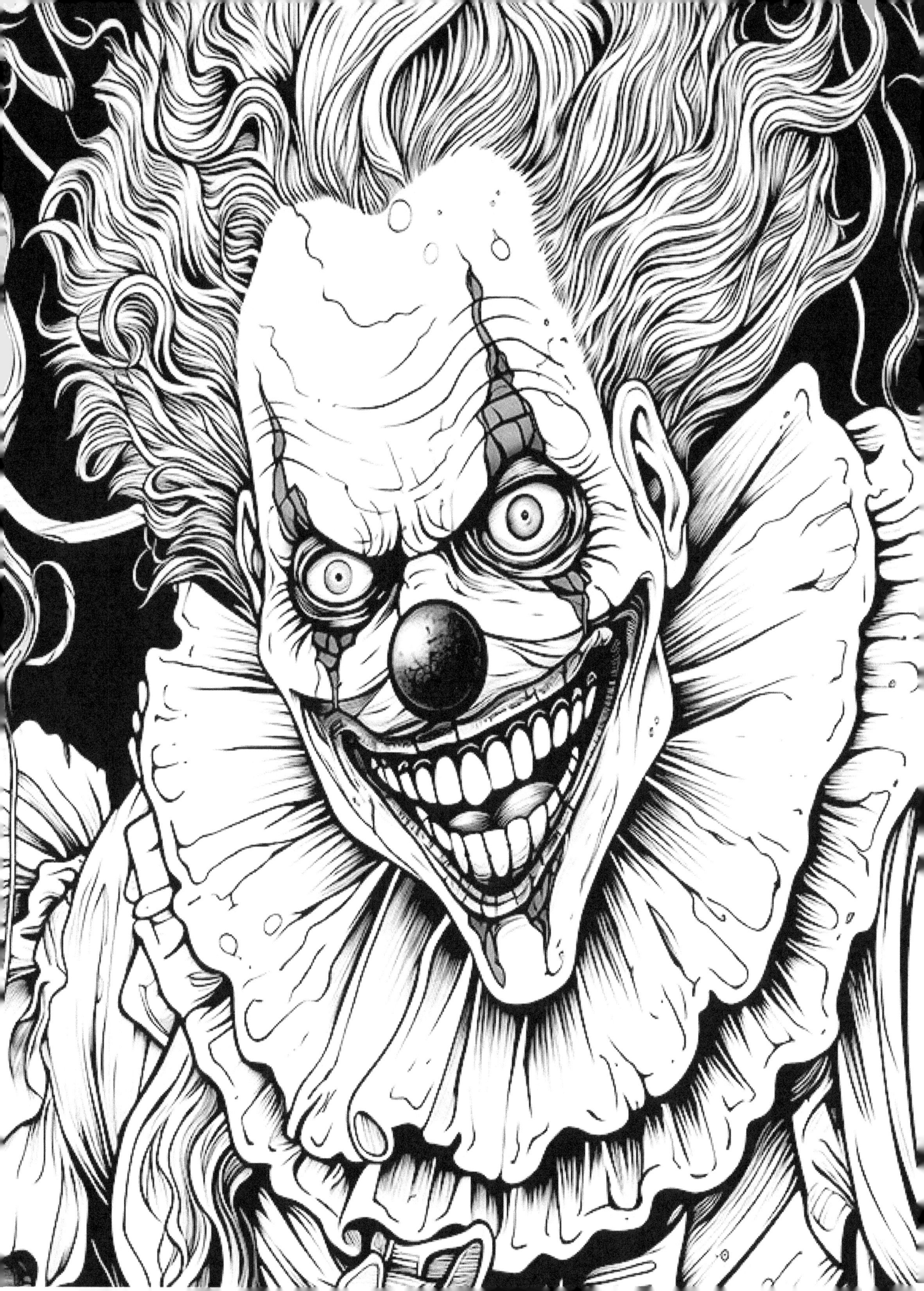

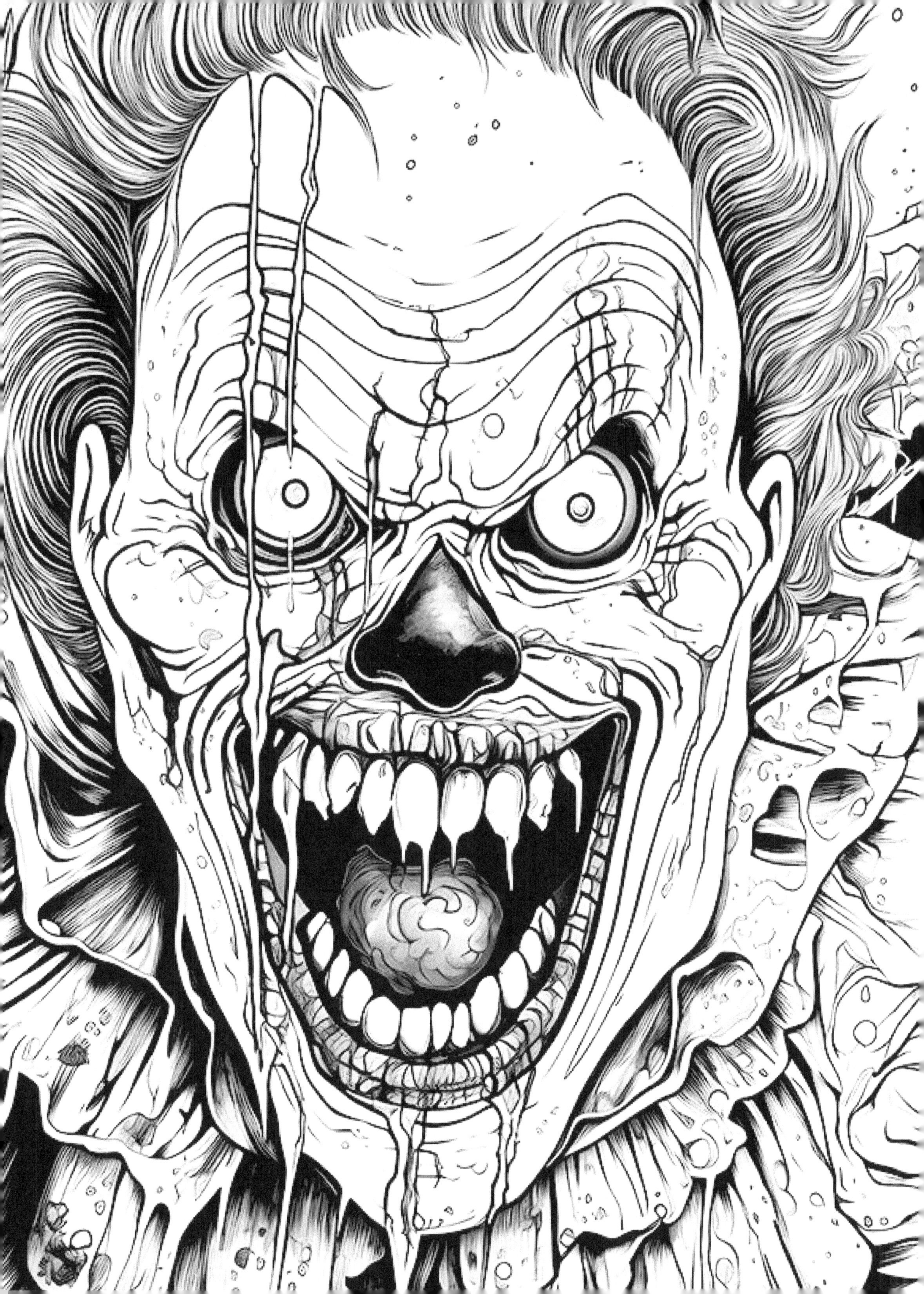

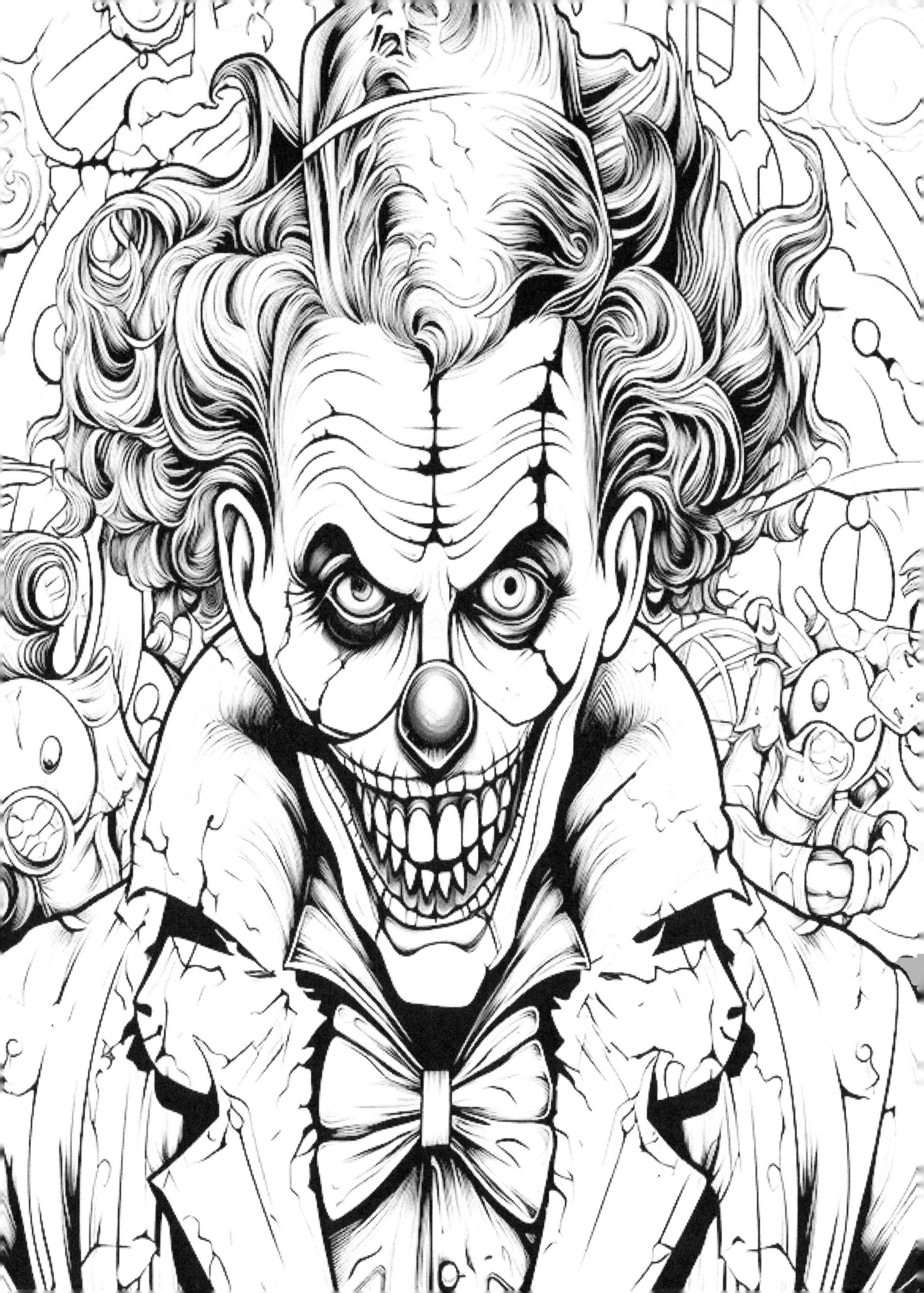

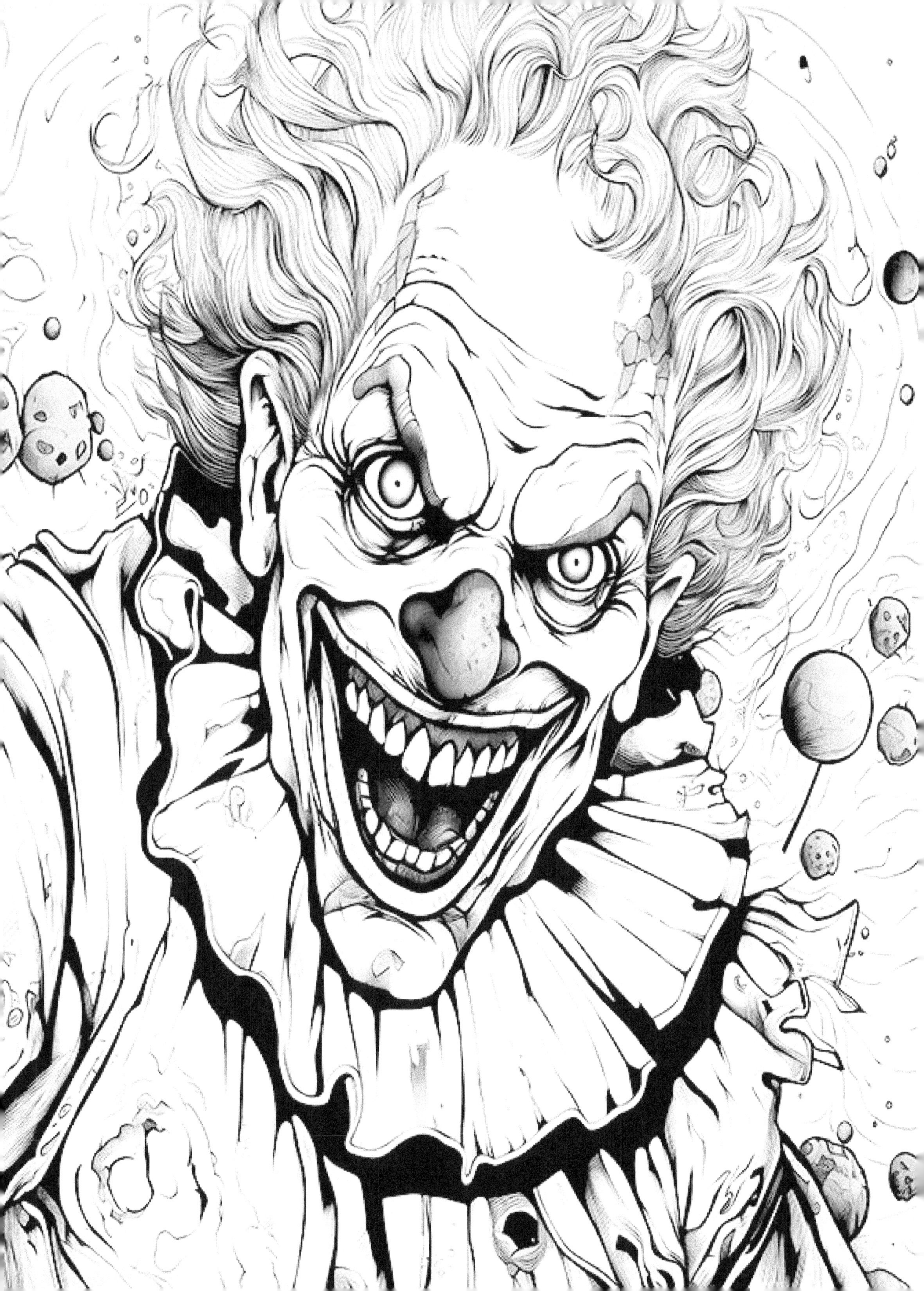

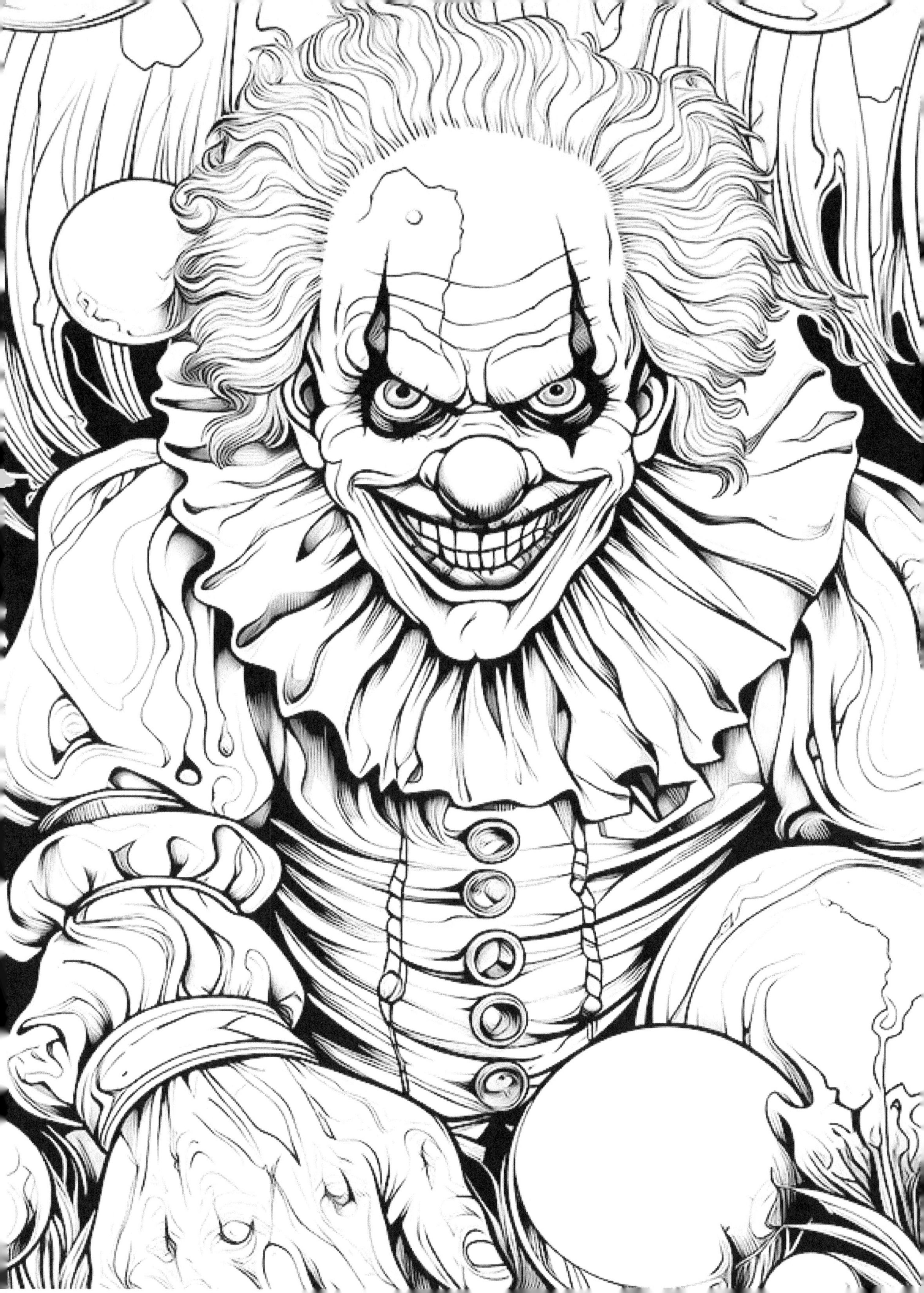

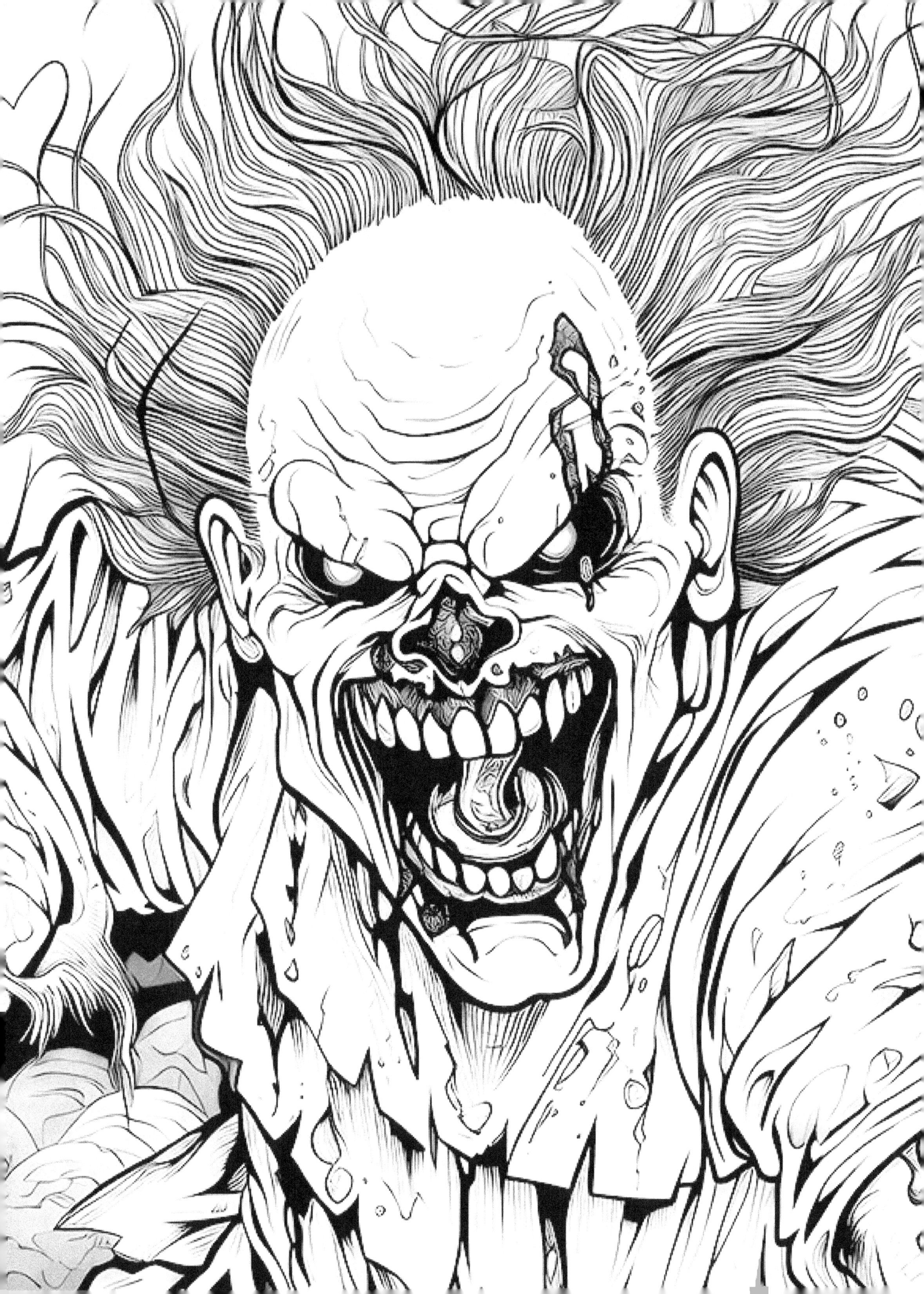

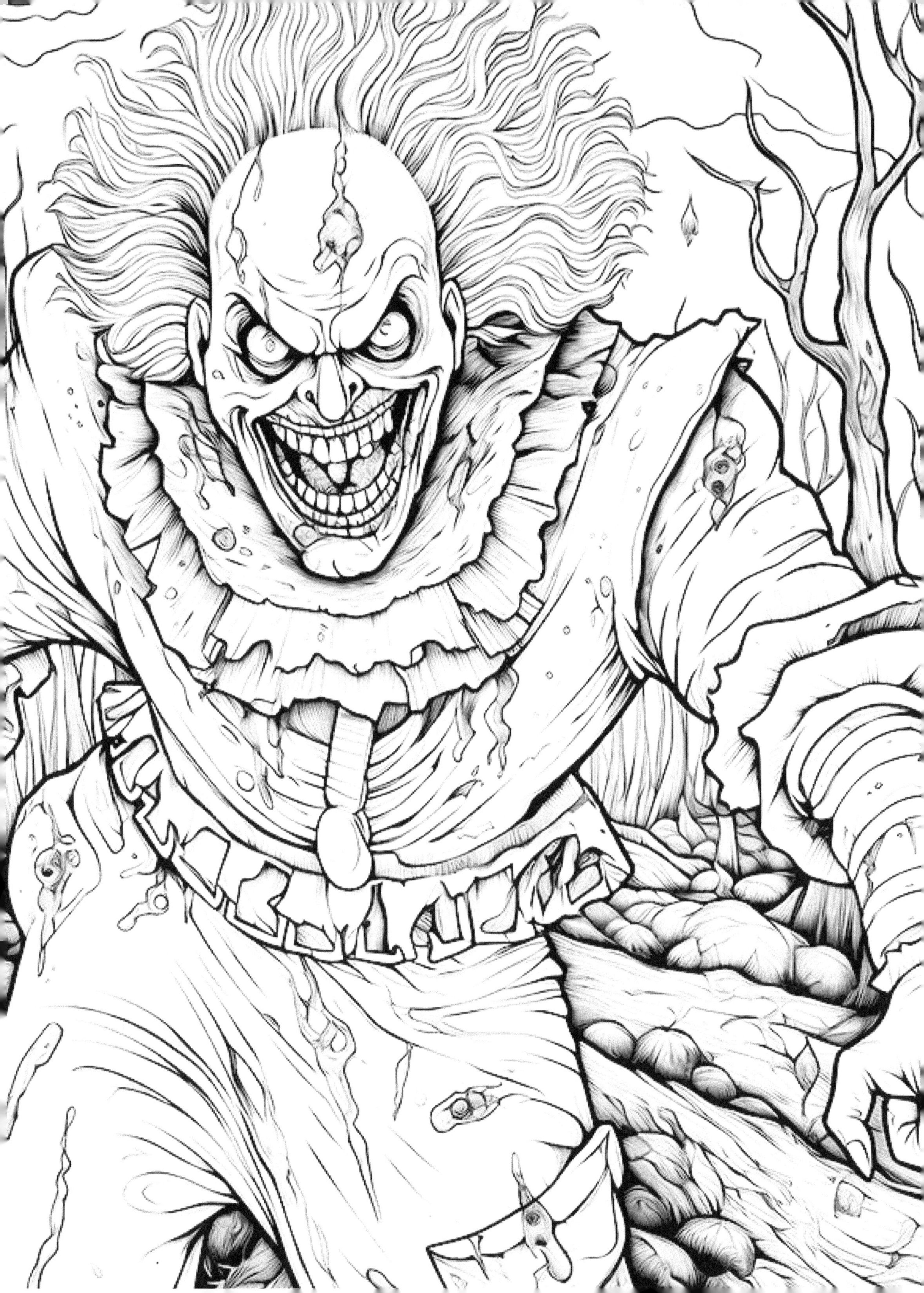

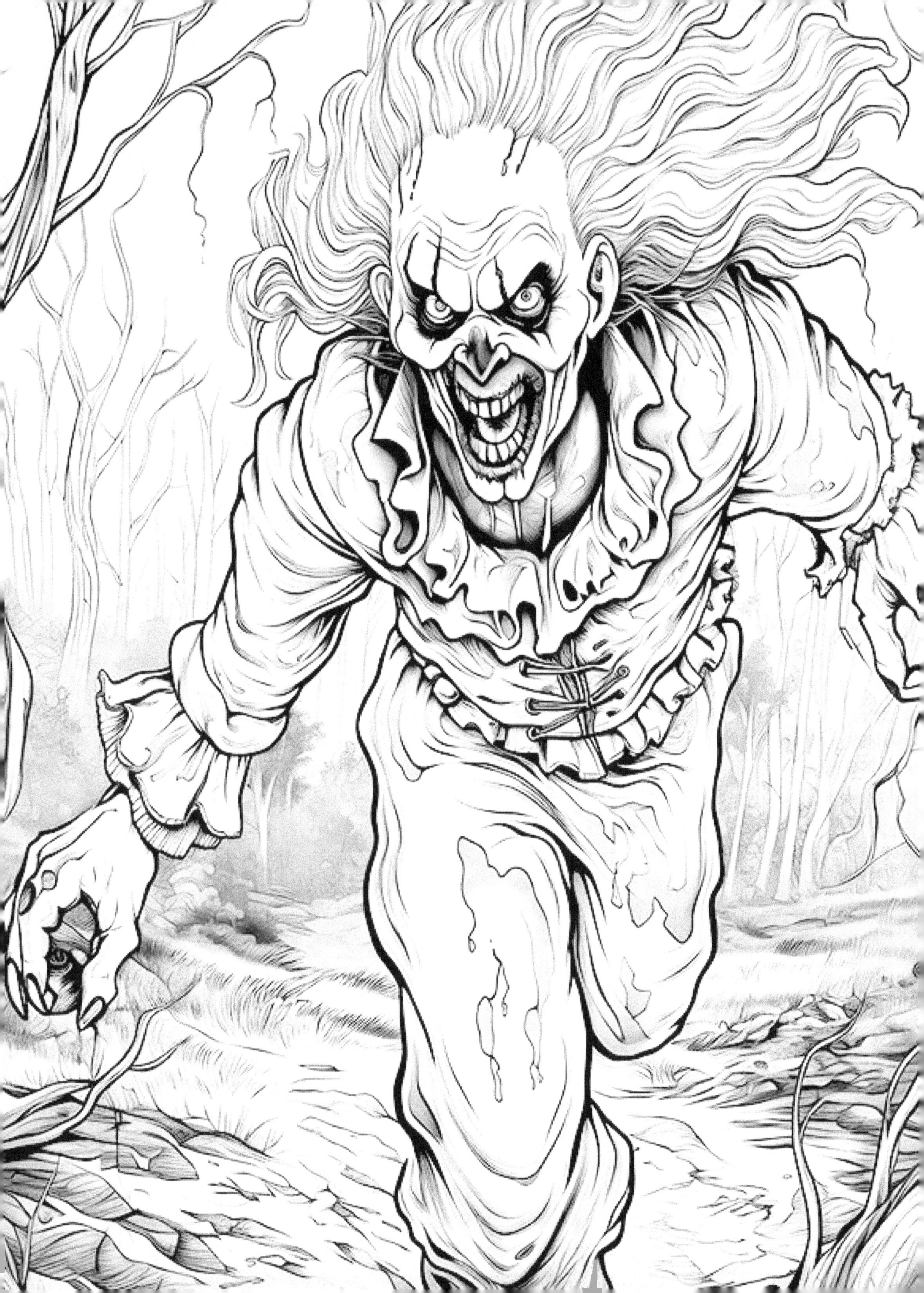

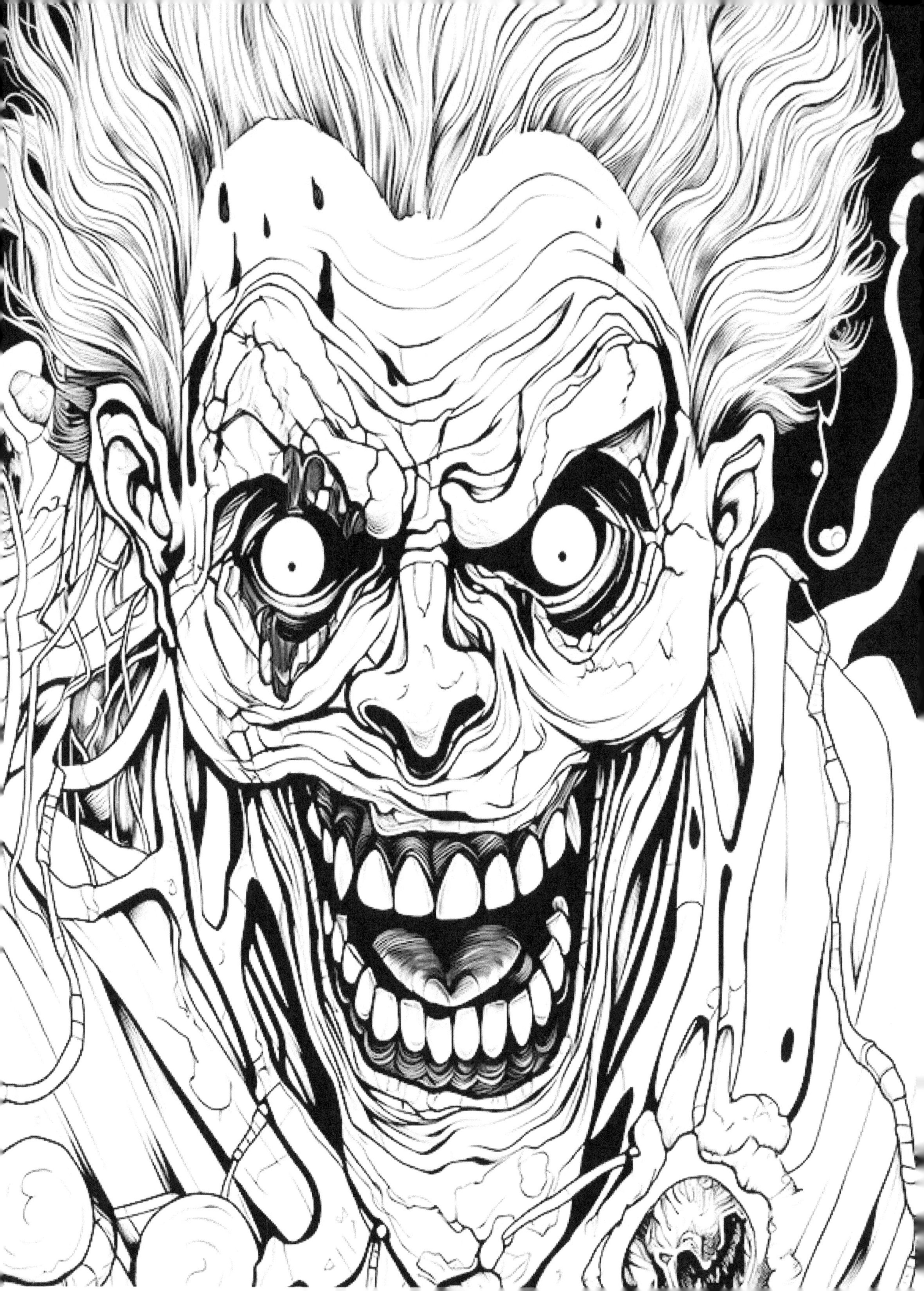

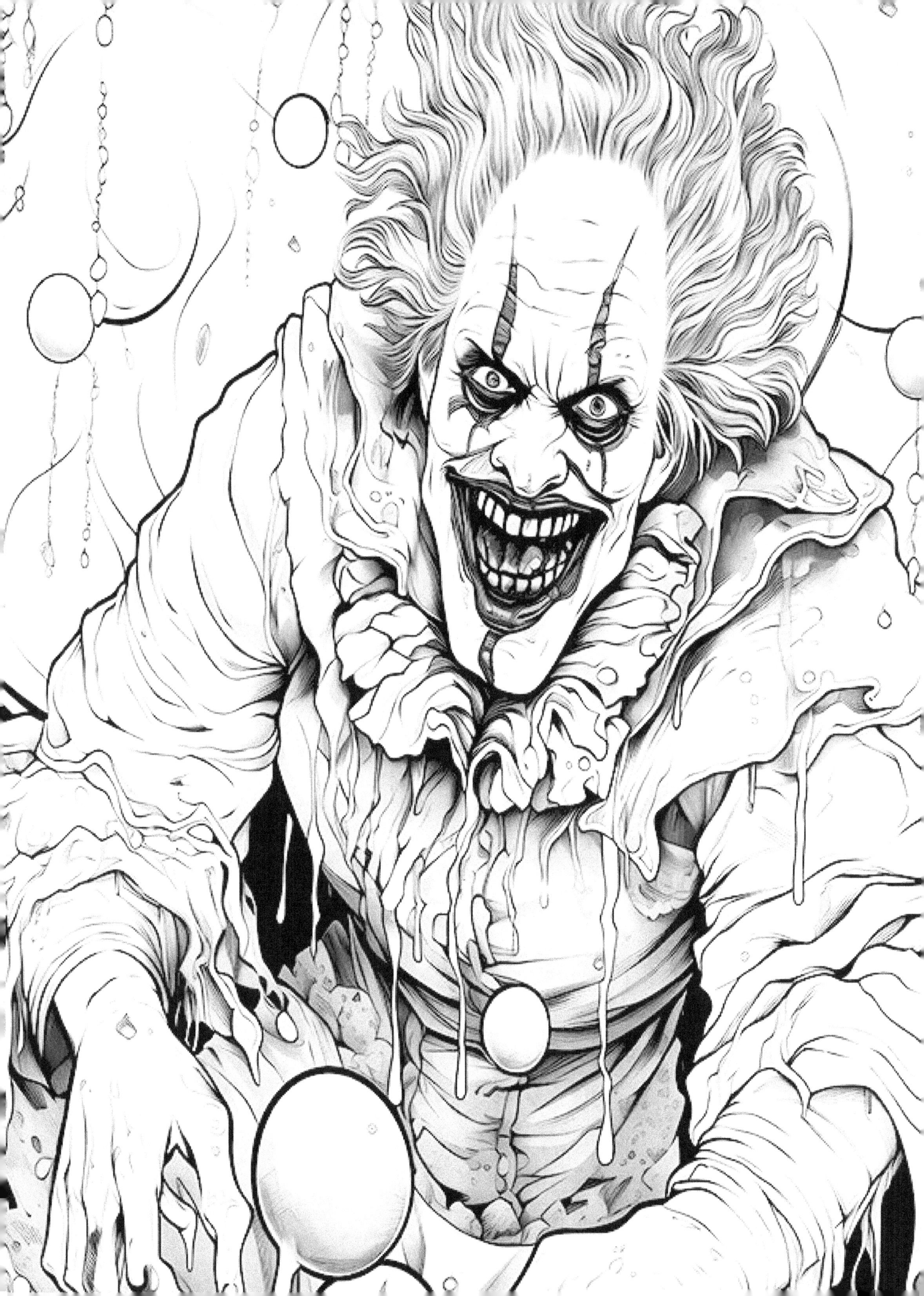

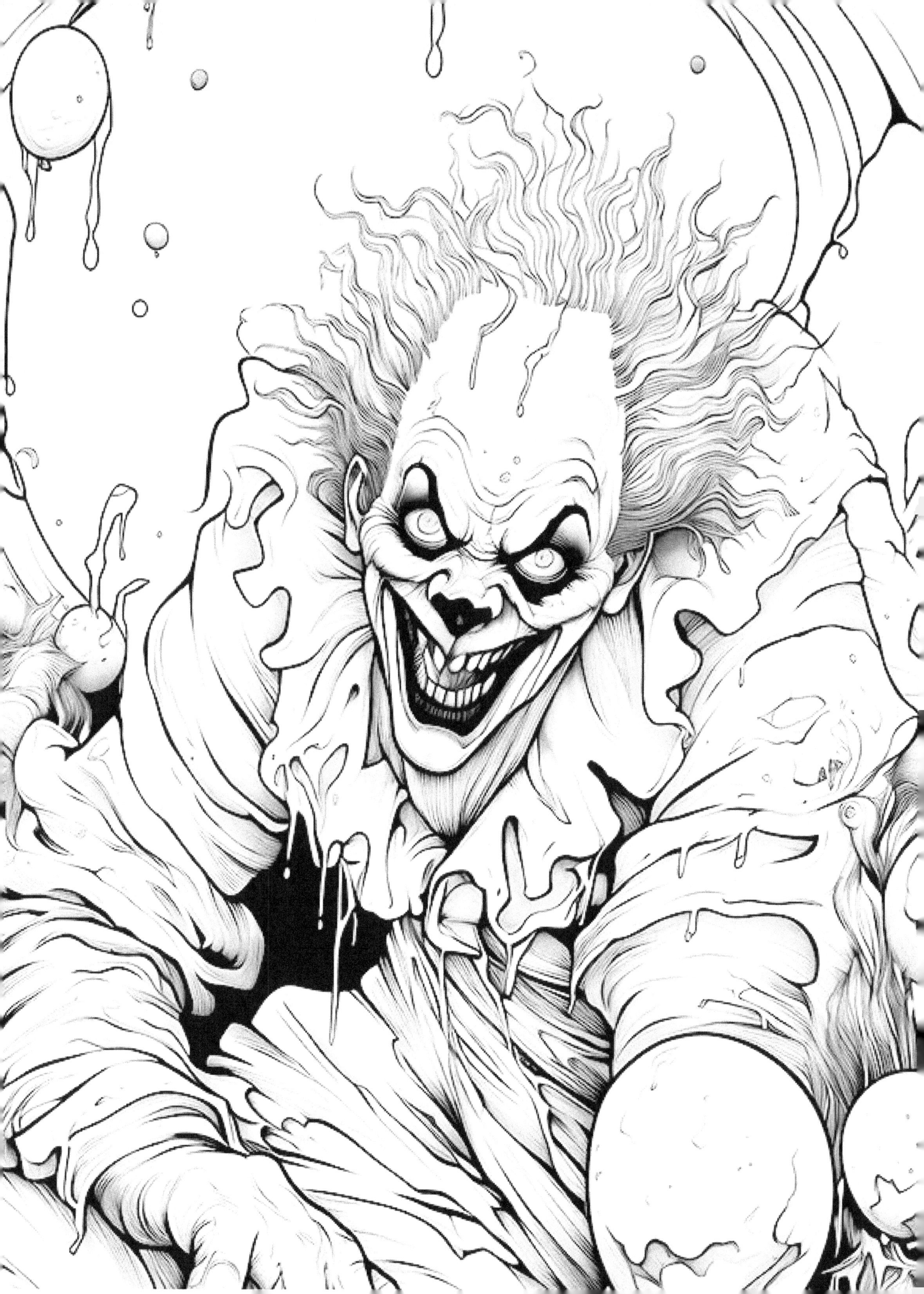

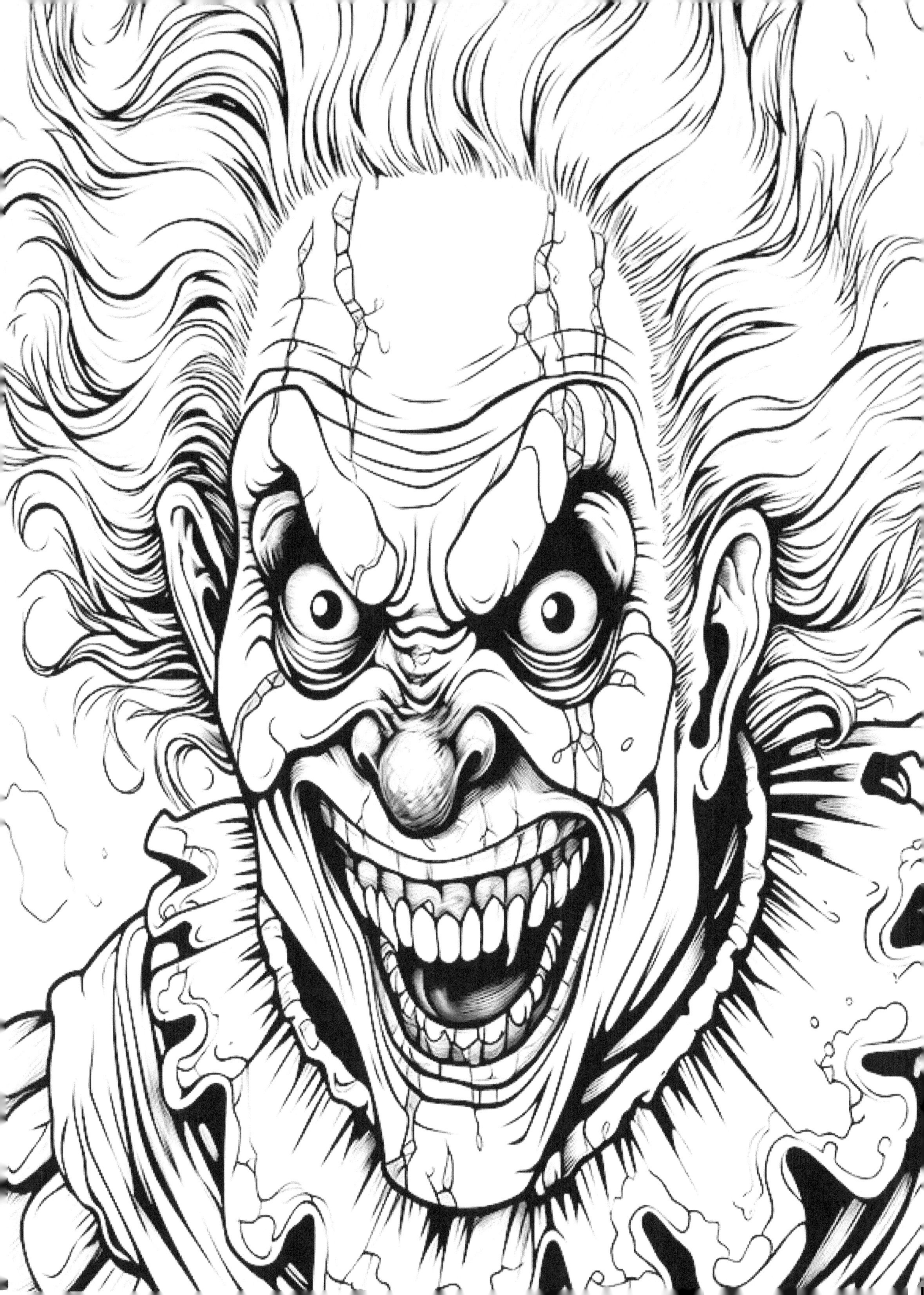

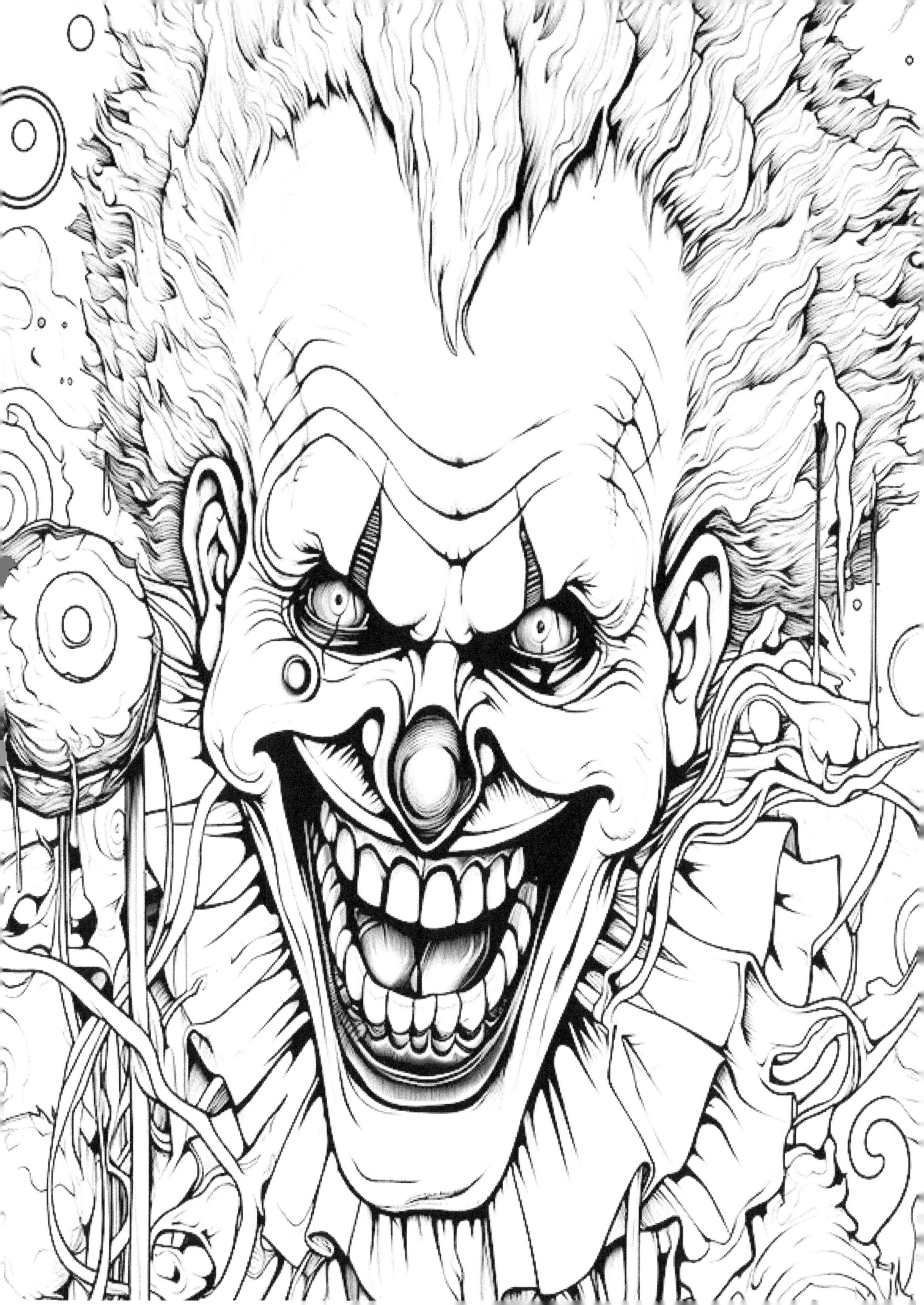

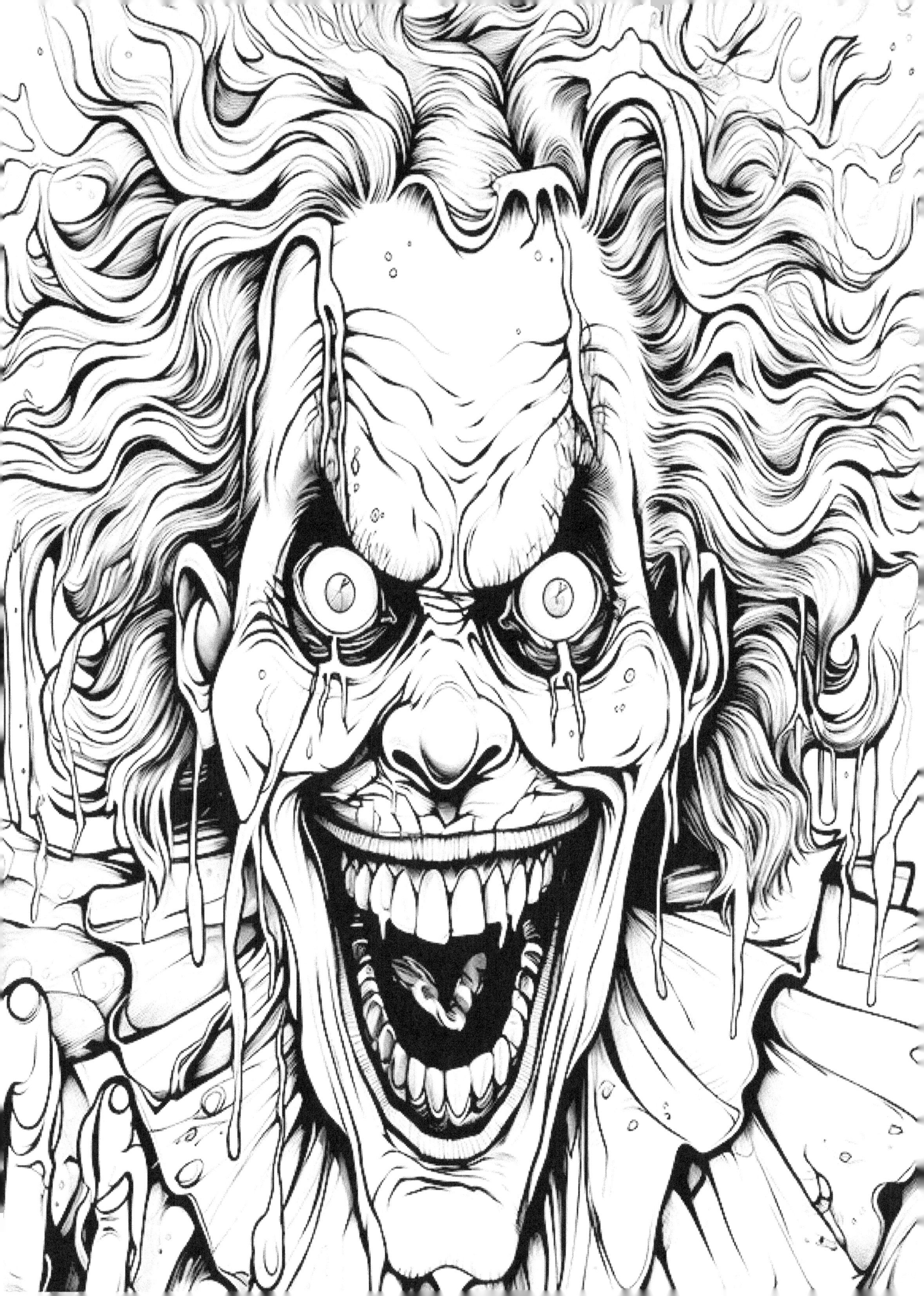

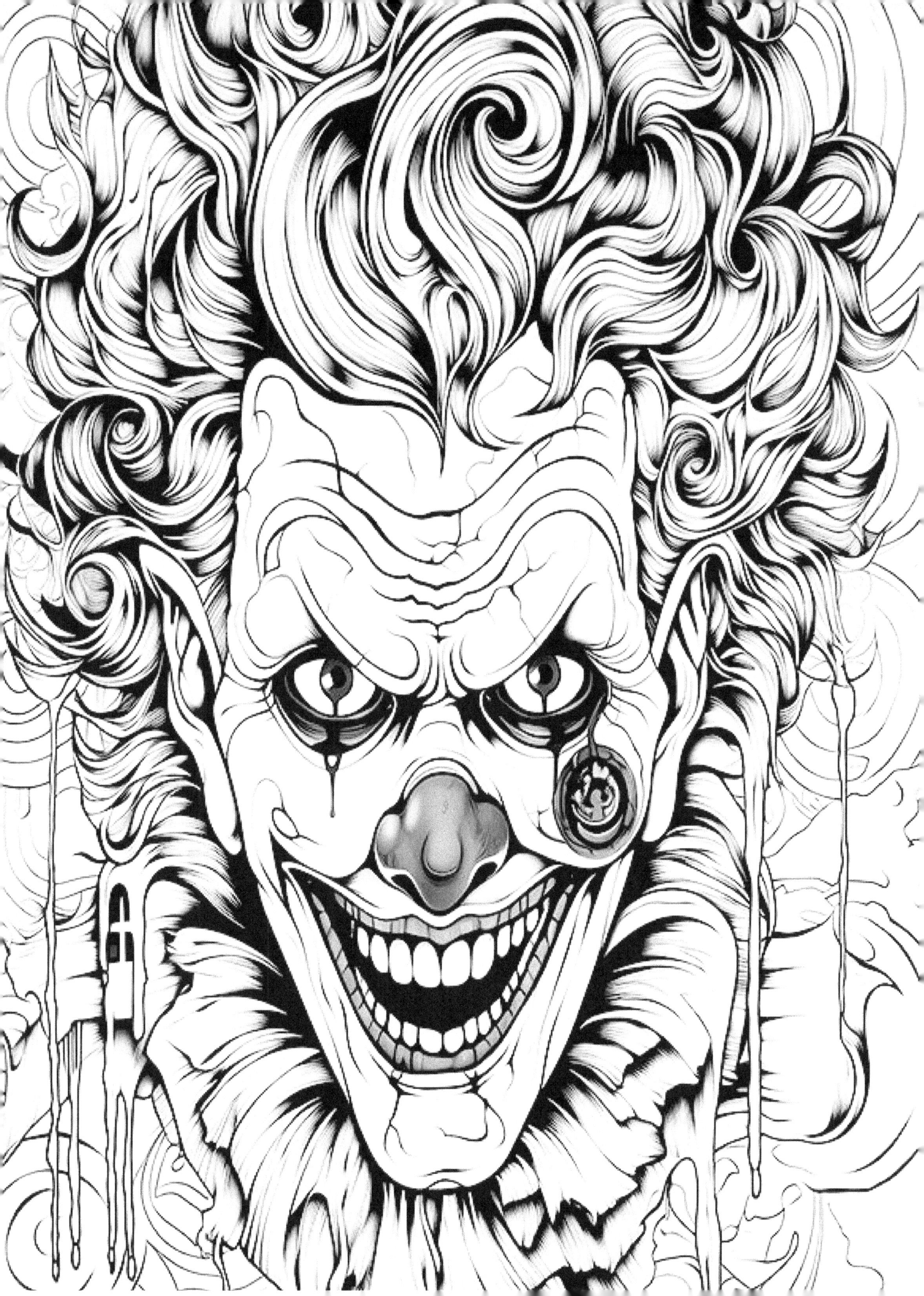

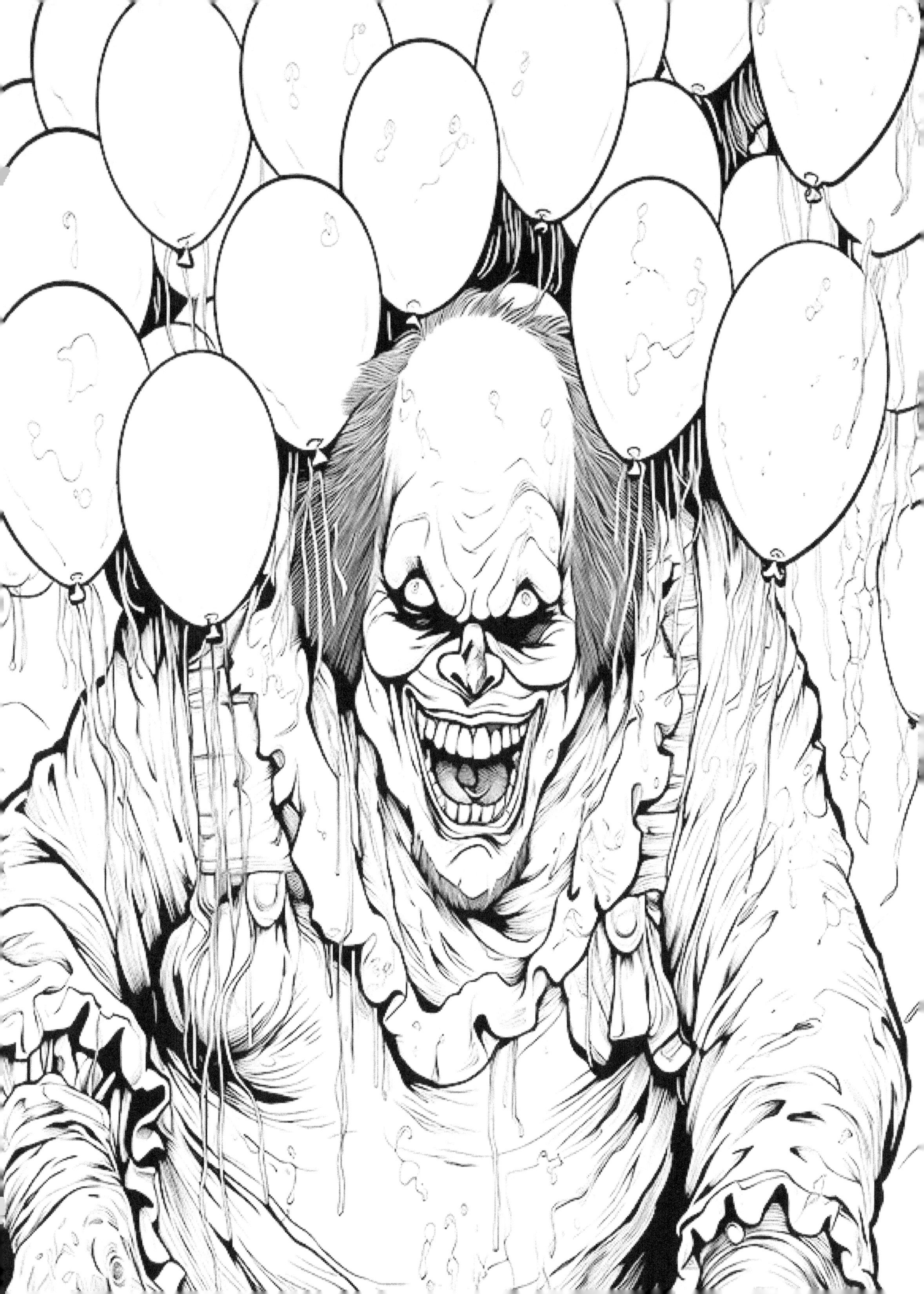

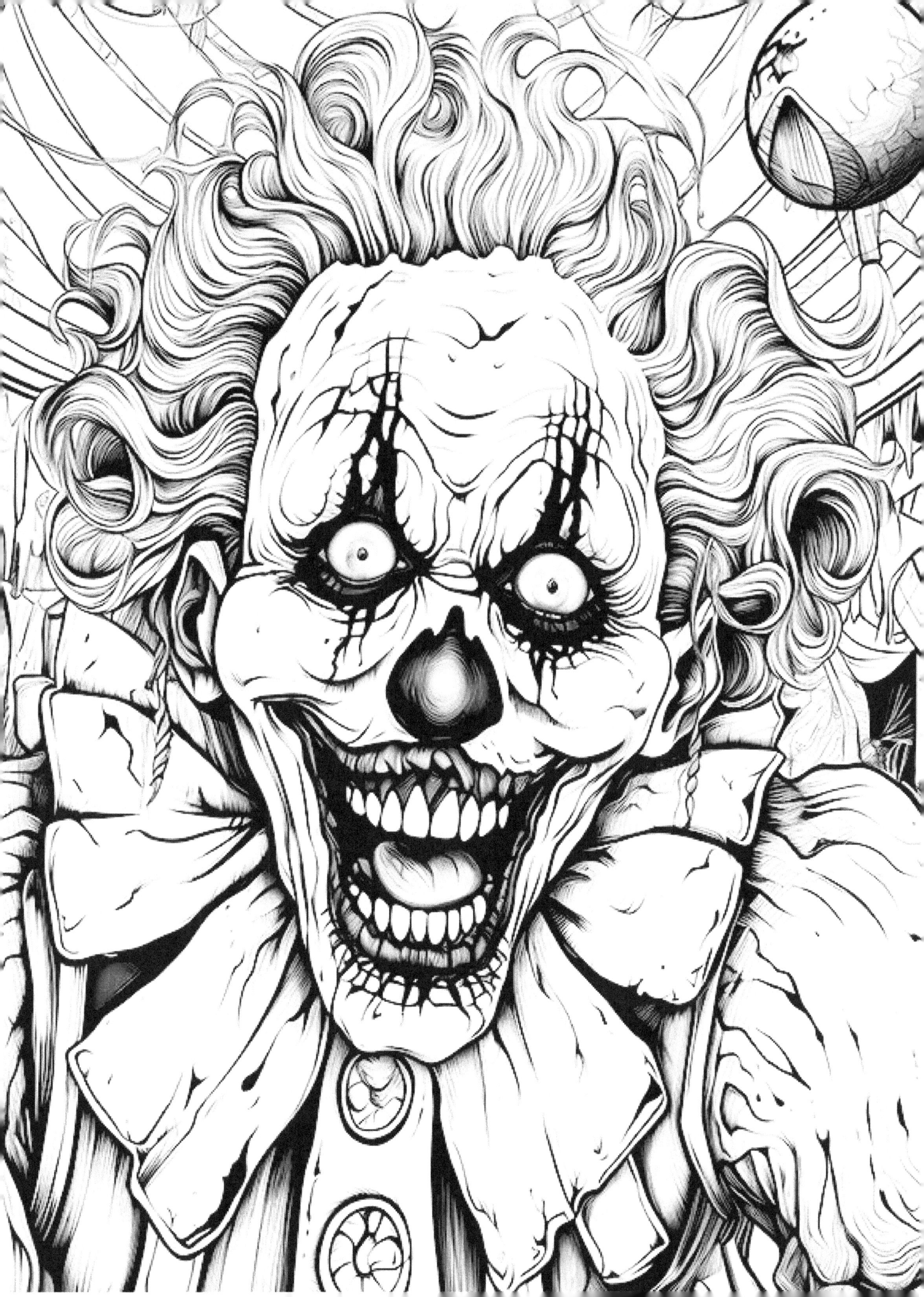

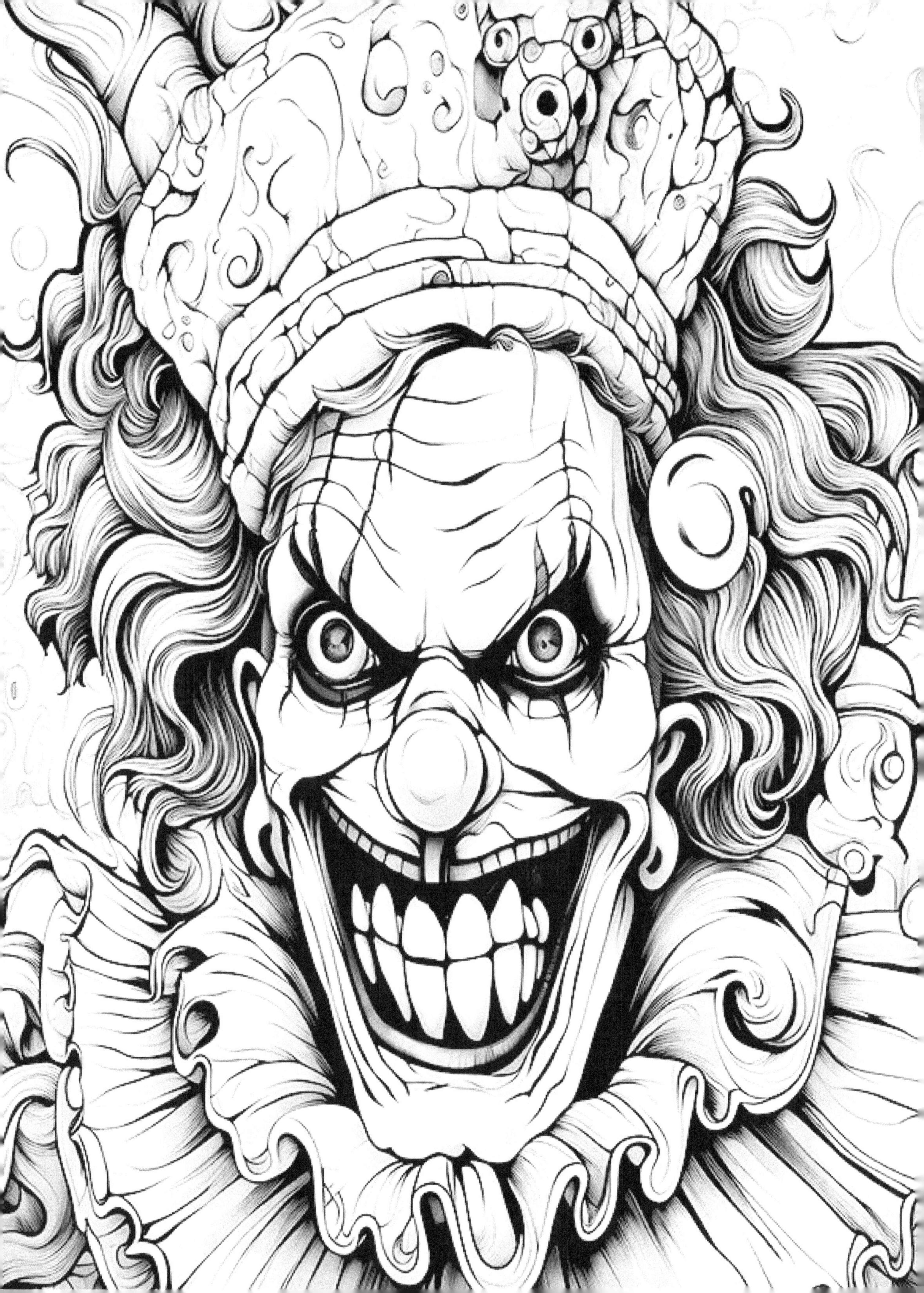

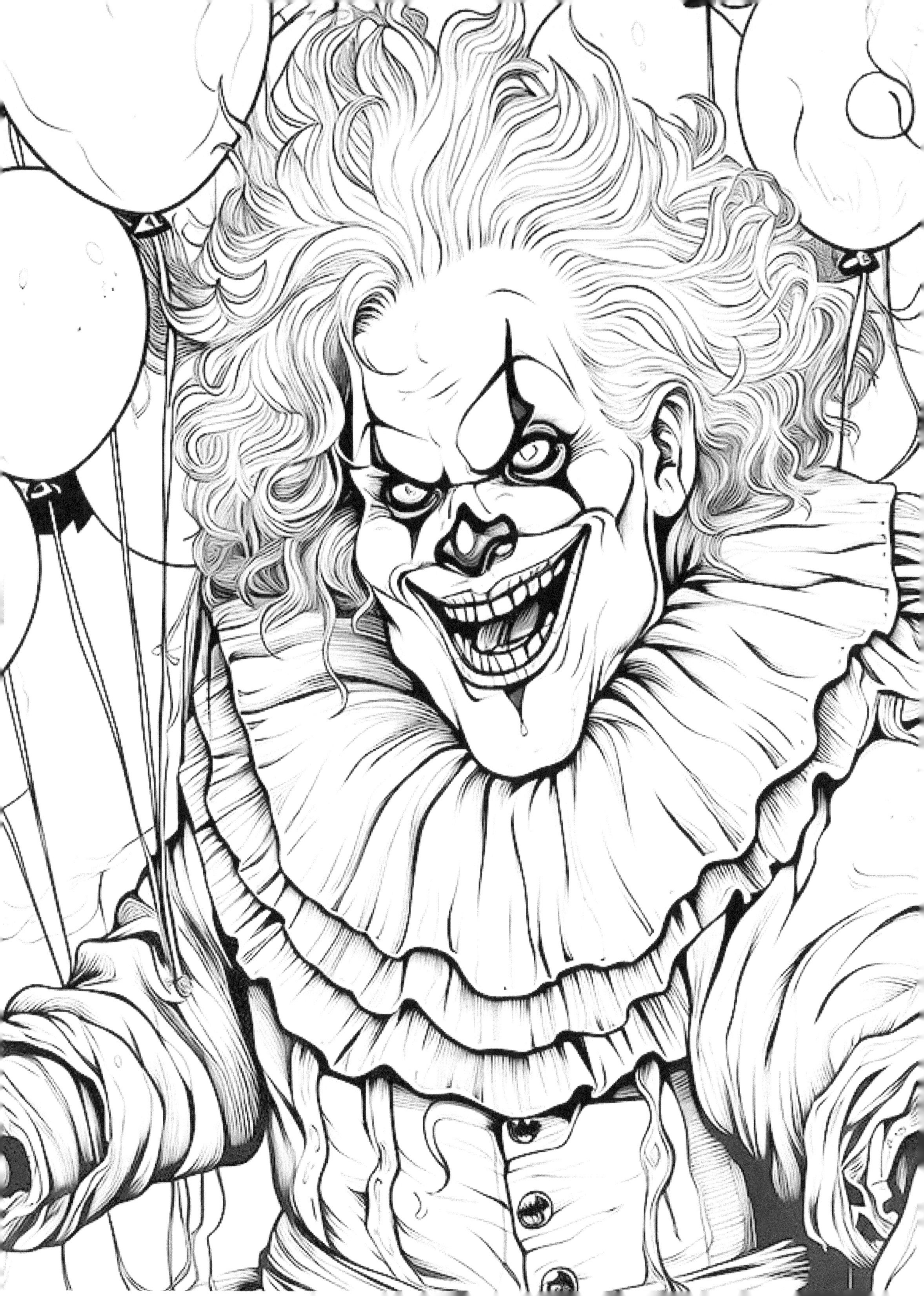

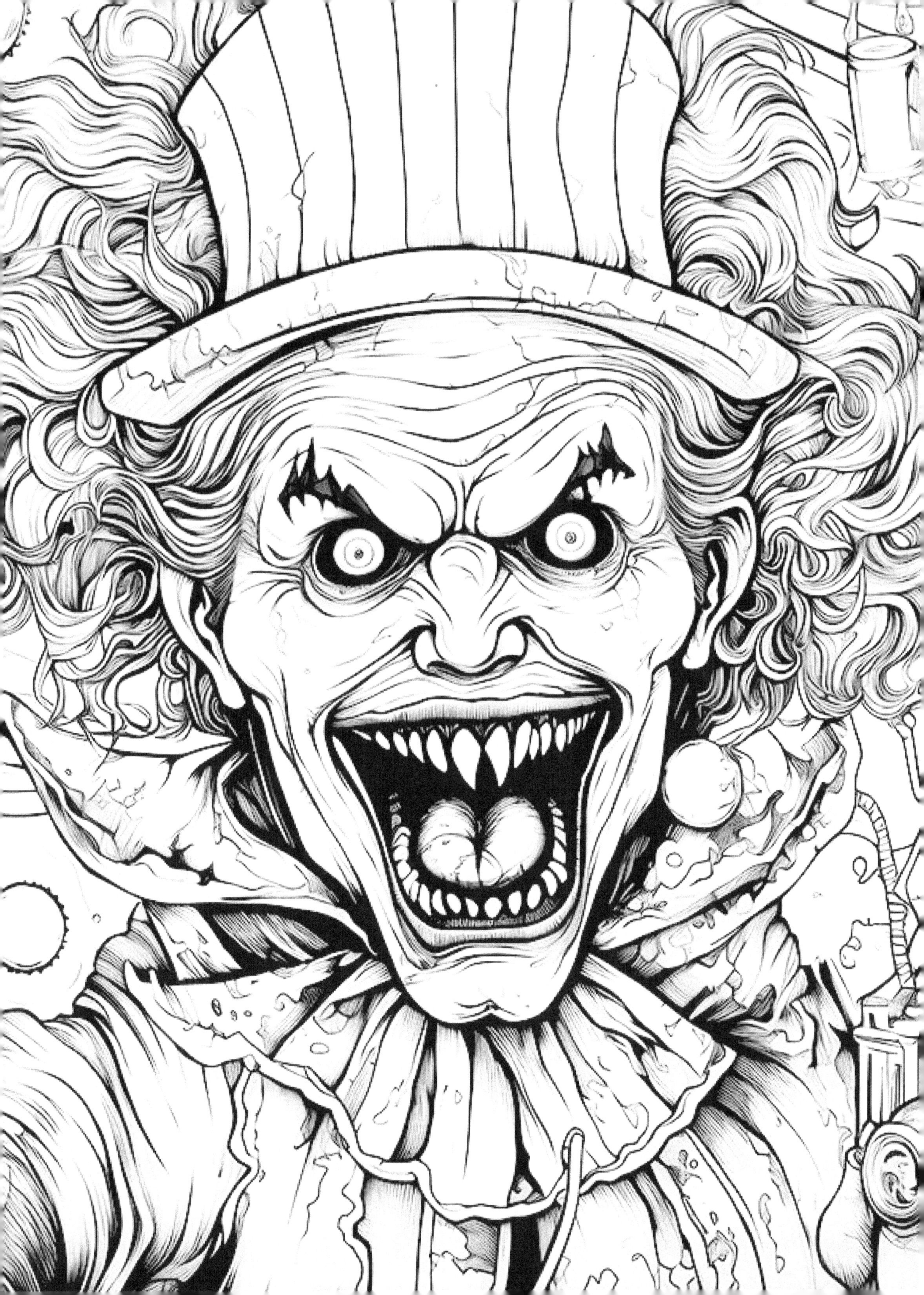

www.ingramcontent.com/pod-product-compliance
Lightning Source LLC
Chambersburg PA
CBHW081135290526
45795CB00006B/2251
9798879908817